Date Due

POEMS

In poems, our earth's wonders
Are windowed through
    Words

A good poem must haunt the heart
And be heeded by the head of the
    Hearer

With a wave of words, a poet can
Change his feelings into cool, magical, mysterious
    Mirages

Without poetry our world would be
Locked within itself—no longer enchanted by the poet's
    Spell.

                Peter Kelso
                Age 11
                Australia
                Taken from
                Richard Lewis's *Miracles*

poetry
in the
elementary
school

VIRGINIA WITUCKE

Purdue University

Pose Lamb
Consulting Editor
Purdue University

WM. C. BROWN COMPANY PUBLISHERS
Dubuque, Iowa

literature for children

Pose Lamb
Consulting Editor
Purdue University

Storytelling and Creative Drama—*Dewey W. Chambers, University of the Pacific, Stockton, California*

Illustrations in Children's Books—*Patricia Cianciolo, Michigan State University*

Enrichment Ideas—*Ruth Kearney Carlson, California State College at Hayward*

History and Trends—*Margaret C. Gillespie, Marquette University*

Poetry in the Elementary School—*Virginia Witucke, Purdue University*

Its Discipline and Content—*Bernice Cullinan, New York University*

Children's Literature in the Curriculum—*Mary Montebello, State University of New York at Buffalo*

Copyright © 1970 by
Wm. C. Brown Company Publishers

ISBN 0–697–06206–6

Library of Congress Catalog Card Number: 74-104987

Third Printing, 1973

Printed in the United States of America.

contents

foreword

This series of books came to be because of the editor's conviction that most textbooks about literature for children had not been written for elementary teachers, regardless of the anticipated audience suggested by the titles. The words, *Literature for Children*, preceding each individual title indicate not only the respect for the field held by the authors and the editor but our evaluation of the importance of this type of literature, worthy of consideration along with other categories or classifications of English literature. However, it is *what happens* through books, and the *uses* of literature which are of concern to the authors of this series, as well as the provision of an historical perspective and some knowledge of the writer's and the illustrator's crafts. Our work, then, is directed primarily to the elementary classroom teacher who wants to design and implement an effective program of literature for children.

Because entire books have been devoted to specific topics, for example, the history of literature for children, it is hoped that such topics are covered in greater depth than usual. They are not merely books *about* children's literature; the focus in this series is on helping teachers see what literature for children has been, the direction or directions pointed by scholars in the field, and some ways in which a teacher can share with children the excitement and joy of reading. The authors have tried to share with teachers and prospective teachers their enthusiasm for children's literature, today's and yesterday's; for an unenthusiastic teacher, though well-informed, will not communicate enthusiasm to his pupils.

The author of each book was selected, first because he has demonstrated this enthusiasm in his teaching and writing, and secondly because of his competence in the field of children's literature in general. It is hoped that the thoroughness and depth with which each topic has been explored and the expertise which each author has brought to a topic in which he has a particular interest will serve as sufficient justifications for such a venture.

Children's literature courses are among the most popular courses in the professional sequence at many colleges and universities. It is rewarding and exciting to re-enter the world of literature for children, to experience again the joy of encountering a new author or of renewing acquaintance with a favorite author or a character created by an author.

The editor and the authors of this series have tried to capture the magic that is literature for children and to provide some help for teachers who want to share that *magic with children.*

It is generally admitted that poetry has not received the attention it deserves in the literature program of the elementary school. Huck and Kuhn note that most Americans don't read poetry, and that change in attitudes toward poetry must begin in the elementary school. They add: "And yet the schools have failed miserably in their presentation of poetry! Teachers have probably done more to mitigate against it than they have ever done to promote a love for it."[1]

Virginia Witucke's positive attitudes toward poetry are evident in this book. Her enthusiasm may help the reader whose feelings about poetry are best described as neutral. It seems clear that teachers do communicate attitudes as well as information, and prior to reading *Poetry in the Elementary School,* it is suggested that the reader carefully examine his own attitudes. What are the most honest answers for these questions:

— What kind of poetry do I enjoy? Why?
— Where and how did my attitudes toward poetry develop?
— What changes will have to occur in my thinking and feeling in order to work with my pupils in this realm?

The author discusses at some length strategies which might be used by a teacher who is interested in and concerned about generating attitude change in his pupils—the boys who believe poetry is "silly" and "effeminate" and girls who believe rhyme and meter are the essence of poetry.

The reader will find much to consider, much to which he will react emotionally and in a very creative and personal sense. For, as the author writes, "The most important aspect of poetry is its ability to say something to a reader."

Pose Lamb, Editor

---

[1]Charlotte Huck and Doris Young Kuhn, *Children's Literature in the Elementary School.* 2d ed. (New York: Holt, Rinehart & Winston, 1968).

preface

The invitation to do a book on poetry was greeted with both apprehension and excitement. Apprehension—because the writer is not an "expert" on poetry, and because there was only limited time in which to work. Excitement—because this afforded her an opportunity to communicate about one of her firm convictions to people who are in a position to bring children and poetry together. This conviction is her belief that poetry is for all children.

The writer has been trying to recall when and how she became receptive to poetry. Like most people, she can remember being turned away from poetry by those who were supposed to have been striving for quite the opposite effect. Somewhere in her development as an elementary teacher, and then as a librarian, she became an active user of poetry with children. Their response carried her farther into the realm of poetry and convinced her that poetry *is* for everyone.

The writer's approach stems from this background. She sees this book as a starting point for the adult working with children. Whatever the reader's field, poetry has something to offer. It is hoped that those readers who are indifferent or hostile to poetry will reopen the door that they have closed. Those who already love poetry but who don't know children's poetry may be delighted to discover what is available. While the writer will indicate further sources for reading in depth on poetry as a literary genre, she must disclaim any attempt to be scholarly and admit that her primary aim is to help make the reader an enthusiastic user of poetry.

This book is written for the adult who is now, or soon will be working with children. The aim of *Poetry in the Elementary School* is to give a taste of poetry for children, a feeling for it, and some information about it. Suggestions for using poetry with children are an important part of the book.

Throughout the text, the word "teacher" will be used as a convenient (and often accurate) term for the person working with children. Actually, the user of this book may very well not be a classroom teacher, but a librarian (media specialist), a parent, a youth group leader, a religious educator, a teacher of a special subject, a principal, a school volunteer, a recreation director, etc.

The writer's original aim was to include lots of children's poetry. Not to do so seemed like teaching cooking without providing ingredients. Legal and financial restrictions, however, resulted in the necessity of including relatively few poems. Therefore, the reader will find it necessary to accompany the reading of this book with the exploration of several books of children's poems. (See Selected References in Chapter 2.)

Poetry is too humanistic to be reducible to a definitive science. This is its glory and the novice's frustration. The reader is cautioned not to stop with one book about poetry—every book that is read will give a new viewpoint. Practically every opinion will have a counter-opinion somewhere.

Just as a tour guide can enhance sightseeing, books about poetry can provide information and develop awareness. But the interaction between the tourist and what he sees is the real reason for taking the tour, and poems are the real aim now, not theory.

Likewise, there is great diversity and argument concerning the best means of bringing children and poetry together. The ultimate decision will be the reader's, based on his own knowledge, openness, creativity, and perceptiveness.

It is the author's hope that this book can be for many the beginning of a lifetime quest and pleasure.

V. W.

acknowledgment

Grateful acknowledgment is given for permission to use the following copyrighted material:

"Poems," "Death," and "Hurting" from *Miracles* by Richard Lewis, copyright 1966 by Richard Lewis. Reprinted by permission of Simon & Schuster, Inc.

"Up the Trail" and "Afternoon" from *Little Herder in Summer* by Ann Clark; "Meetings" from *Little Herder in Spring* by Ann Clark. Reprinted by permission of the Bureau of Indian Affairs, U. S. Department of the Interior.

"Magic" from *The Moon and a Star*, copyright 1965 by Myra Cohn Livingston. Reprinted by permission of Harcourt Brace Jovanovich, Inc.

"Tree Song" from *The Wizard in the Well*, copyright 1966 by Harry Behn. Reprinted by permission of Harcourt Brace Jovanovich, Inc.

"Feelings about Words" from *Words, Words, Words* by Mary O'Neill, copyright 1966 by Mary O'Neill. Reprinted by permission of Doubleday & Company, Inc.

"Skyscrapers" by Rachel Field from *Taxis and Toadstools*, copyright 1926 by Doubleday & Company, Inc. Reprinted by permission of Doubleday & Company, Inc.

"Robert, Who Is Often a Stranger to Himself" from *Bronzeville Boys and Girls* by Gwendolyn Brooks, copyright 1956 by Gwendolyn Brooks Blakely. Reprinted by permission of Harper & Row, Publishers.

"Snowflakes fall to earth" from *A Cloud of Summer* by Doris Johnson. Text copyright 1967, by Doris Johnson. Reprinted by permission of Follett Publishing Company.

"The Warning" from *Verse* by Adelaide Crapsey, copyright 1934. Reprinted by permission of Alfred A. Knopf, Inc.

Particular thanks are extended to Frances Bussard and the fifth grade class at Riverview School, Elkhart, Indiana, where Mrs. Bussard was a student-teacher in the spring of 1969. The pupils' poems are published for the first time in this book.

"Outside" by Julie App.
"Block Busters" by Bill Bohinc.
"Sunset" by Shirley Chapman.
"Baby" by Michael Fahlbeck.
"About School" by Duane Krauter.
"Summer" by Sherri Mahan.
"Sun" by Mark Scher.
"The Sea" by Cristina Truex.
"Pepper" by Annette Warren.

Also used were the following works which are in the public domain:
"Introduction" and "Spring" from *Songs of Innocence* by William Blake.
"Jabberwocky" from *Through the Looking-Glass* by Lewis Carroll.
"There Was an Old Man with a Beard" and "The Nutcrackers and the Sugar-Tongs" from *The Complete Nonsense Book* by Edward Lear.
"A Pin Has a Head" from *Sing-Song* by Christina Rossetti.
"From a Railway Carriage" from *A Child's Garden of Verses* by Robert Louis Stevenson.

chapter 1

what is poetry?

Right now, what comes to the reader's mind when he hears the word "poetry"? Iambic pentameter? Rhythm? Joy? Having to memorize and recite thirty lines? A particular poem? The recognition of his own life in the poem of another? A. A. Milne? Bearded poet in sandals? A happy afternoon with a book of poems? The ultimate and only interpretation of Robert Frost, as revealed by an English teacher? Rhyme? A jolt received from the poem written by a pessimist? A visual image of the way a poem looks on a page? *A Child's Garden of Verses*? The memory of a dramatization of *Spoon River Anthology*? Something that's perennially ignored? Literature with a capital L?

What is poetry, especially children's poetry? Whatever it is, it doesn't fit neatly into a definition.

Traditional Verse

Poetry starts with the traditional nursery (Mother Goose) rhymes which all of us heard when we were very young; they were sung or recited or chanted to us. Can the reader ever remember not knowing rhymes like these?

> Hey diddle, diddle,
> The cat and the fiddle,
> The cow jumped over the moon,
>   The little dog laughed
>   To see such sport,
> And the dish ran away with the spoon.

> Humpty Dumpty sat on a wall,
> Humpty Dumpty had a great fall.
> All the king's horses and all the king's men
> Couldn't put Humpty together again.

A second grader offered this version:

> Humpty Dumpty sat on a wall,
> Humpty Dumpty had a great fall.
> All the king's horses and all the king's men
> Had scrambled eggs.

Jack and Jill and the well are familiar, but their subsequent adventures may not be.

> Jack and Jill
> Went up the hill,
> To fetch a pail of water;
> Jack fell down,
> And broke his crown,
> And Jill came tumbling after.
>
> Then up Jack got,
> And home did trot,
> As fast as he could caper;
> To old Dame Dob,
> Who patched his nob
> With vinegar and brown paper.
>
> When Jill came in,
> How she did grin
> To see Jack's paper plaster;
> Her mother, vexed,
> Did whip her next,
> For laughing at Jack's disaster.
>
> Now Jack did laugh
> And Jill did cry,
> But her tears did soon abate;
> Then Jill did say,
> That they should play
> At see-saw across the gate.

We heard our first rhymes within our family group when the adults very likely played related games with us. Typical of these verses is the following which points out parts of the face.

> Bo peeper,
> Nose dreeper,
> Chin chopper,
> White lopper,
> Red rag,
> And little gap.

Contacts with other children and at school expanded the number and kinds of verses we knew. We learned finger plays, facts as well as superstitions, tongue twisters, dire sayings, and hyperbole.

Two little blackbirds, sitting on a hill,
One named Jack and one named Jill.
Fly away, Jack! Fly away, Jill!
Come back, Jack! Come back, Jill!

Star light, star bright,
First star I've seen tonight,
I wish I may, I wish I might,
Have the wish I wish tonight.

Fee, fi, fo, fum,
I smell the blood of an Englishman:
Be he alive or be he dead,
I'll grind his bones to make my bread.

Thirty days hath September,
April, June and November;
All the rest have thirty-one,
Except February alone,
Which has twenty-eight days clear
And twenty-nine in each leap year.

Suddenly swerving, seven small swans
Swam silently southward,
Seeing six swift sailboats
Sailing sedately seaward.

I asked my mother for fifty cents
To see the elephant jump the fence,
He jumped so high that he touched the sky
And never came back till the Fourth of July.

How many rhymes learned painlessly during childhood can the reader still recite? For all the rhymes any one person knows, there are hundreds of others that could as well be shared with children. Iona and Peter Opie's *Oxford Nursery Rhyme Book* has 800 entries. Books such as *The American Mother Goose* and *Rocket in My Pocket* add still more possibilities. The reader is likely to find at least some of the following traditional rhymes, exemplary of the unexplored, new to him.

Snow, snow faster.
Ally-ally blaster.
The old woman's plucking her geese,
Selling the feathers a penny a piece.

Dickery, dickery, dare,
The pig flew up in the air;
The man in brown soon brought him down,
Dickery, dickery, dare.

For want of a nail
    The shoe was lost,
For want of a shoe
    The horse was lost,

For want of a horse
    The rider was lost,
For want of a rider
    The battle was lost,
For want of a battle
    The kingdom was lost,
And all for the want
    Of a horseshoe nail.

There was an old woman tossed up in a basket,
    Seventeen times as high as the moon;
Where she was going I couldn't but ask it,
    For in her hand she carried a broom.
Old woman, old woman, old woman, quoth I,
    Where are you going to up so high?
To brush the cobwebs off the sky!
    May I go with you? Aye, by-and-by.

    The north wind doth blow,
    And we shall have snow,
    And what will poor Robin do then?
        Poor thing!
    He'll sit in a barn,
    And to keep himself warm,
    Will hide his head under his wing.
        Poor thing!

Sneeze on Monday,
Sneeze for danger.
    Sneeze on Tuesday,
    Kiss a stranger.
Sneeze on Wednesday,
Sneeze for a letter.
    Sneeze on Thursday,
    Something better.
Sneeze on Friday,
Sneeze for sorrow.
    Sneeze on Saturday,
    Joy tomorrow.
Sneeze on Sunday,
Company comin'.

    Hector Protector was dressed all in green.
    Hector Protector was sent to the Queen.
    The Queen did not like him,
    No more did the King;
    So Hector Protector was sent home again.[1]

---

[1]See Maurice Sendak's delightful illustrated interpretation of this five-line verse in his book, *Hector Protector*, which demonstrates the work of a really creative mind. Maurice Sendak, *Hector Protector* and *As I Went Over the Water*; two nursery rhymes with pictures (New York: Harper & Row, Publishers, 1965).

Riddles are popular with all ages and are often useful with the child whose attitude toward poetry is negative.

> I saw a fishpond all on fire
> I saw a horse bow to a squire
> I saw a parson twelve feet high
> I saw a cottage near the sky
> I saw a balloon made of lead
> I saw a coffin drop down dead
> I saw two sparrows run a race
> I saw two horses making lace
> I saw a girl just like a cat
> I saw a kitten wear a hat
> I saw a man who saw these too
> And said though strange
> they all were true.[2]

> I'll tell you a story
> About Jack a Nory,
> And now my story's begun;
> I'll tell you another
> Of Jack and his brother,
> And now my story is done.

The cumulative rhyme, as well as one that tells a story, is exemplified by "This Is the House that Jack Built," that starts like this:

> This is the house
>   that Jack built.

> This is the malt
> That lay in the house
>   that Jack built.

> This is the rat,
> That ate the malt
> That lay in the house
>   that Jack built.

and builds, one line at a time, to this:

> This is the horse and the hound and the horn,
> That belonged to the farmer sowing his corn,
> That kept the cock that crowed in the morn,
> That waked the priest all shaven and shorn,
> That married the man all tattered and torn,
> That kissed the maiden all forlorn,
> That milked the cow with the crumpled horn,
> That tossed the dog,
> That worried the cat,
> That killed the rat,
> That ate the malt
> That lay in the house
>   that Jack built.

---

[2]In effect, this is a riddle. Is it as meaningless as it first sounds? Add punctuation marks so that it will make better sense.

For the more mature child who is familiar with nursery rhymes, there are poems that are built on Mother Goose, but that go beyond the well-known rhymes. A notable collection is Frederick Winsor's *The Space Child's Mother Goose,* which parodies the originals in very modern terms.

An interesting recent development is the translation of nursery rhymes from other cultures into English. *The Prancing Pony*[3] (Japan), *Chinese Mother Goose Rhymes,*[4] and *Pajaro-Cu-Cu*[5] are examples. The mood and subjects are quite different from those of our rhymes.

While nursery rhymes have their greatest appeal to the young, carefully selected traditional rhymes have a place throughout the elementary school. Rhythm, subject, simplicity, humor and universality make nursery rhymes popular. They are a part of our heritage which children shouldn't be denied. Yet most are merely verse, not poetry. To limit children to traditional rhymes would be as unfortunate as to deprive children of traditional rhymes.

There is other folklore that is true poetry. This is the lore of the serious adult world. These poems were (and in some places, are) an important part of life—guiding it, giving it form and voice, ornamenting it. Much of this body of language was intended to be chanted or sung. Poems explaining natural phenomena, chants for planting season and time of war, songs of tribal joy, metrical stories for times of rest are often real poetry.

What is poetry? Poetry is traditional verse that is still being passed along by word of mouth. It is verses and poems recorded by folklorists, linguists, anthropologists, and made available in print and sound recording for our enjoyment.

Pre-Twentieth Century Poems

Poetry is verse written long ago for the child audience. William Blake (1757-1827) is generally credited with having been the first to write poems about, and not at, children. His work may cause some difficulty for modern youngsters, but children should be introduced to him. Perhaps the best way is through the two volume edition of *Songs of Innocence.*[6] Ellen Raskin has illustrated the poems in Volume One.

---

[3]Charlotte B. De Forest, *The Prancing Pony.* Adapted into English Verse for Children by Charlotte B. De Forest; with "Kusa-e" illus. by Keiko Hida. (New York: Walker & Co., 1967).

[4]Robert Wyndham, *Chinese Mother Goose Rhymes,* color illus. Ed. Young (Cleveland: World Publishing Co., 1968).

[5]Ingrid Wolf and Gertraut Friches, illus. *Pajaro-Cu-Cu,* animal rhymes from many lands (New York: Atheneum Publishers, 1967).

[6]William Blake, *Songs of Innocence,* music and illus. by Ellen Raskin (New York: Doubleday & Co., 1966).

Using these illustrations more as decorations in the second volume, she has set the poems to music. Urbanized or not, the joy of "Spring" remains and is heightened by an appropriate melody.

SPRING

Sound the Flute!
Now it's mute.
Birds delight
Day and Night;
Nightingale
In the dale,
Lark in Sky,
Merrily,
Merrily, Merrily, to welcome
    in the Year.

Little Boy,
Full of joy;
Little Girl,
Sweet and small;
Cock does crow,
So do you;
Merry voice,
Infant noise,
Merrily, Merrily, to welcome
    in the Year.

Little Lamb,
Here I am;
Come and lick
My white neck;
Let me pull
Your soft Wool;
Let me kiss
Your soft face:
Merrily, Merrily, we welcome
    in the Year.

Early poems for children tended toward the didactic, and yet not too long after Blake, we have the delightfully outrageous Edward Lear (1812-1888).

THE NUTCRACKERS AND THE SUGAR-TONGS

The Nutcrackers sate by a plate on the table;
    The Sugar-tongs sate by a plate at his side;
And the Nutcrackers said, "Don't you wish we were able
    Along the blue hills and green meadows to ride?
Must we drag on this stupid existence forever
    So idle and weary, so full of remorse,
While every one else takes his pleasure, and never
    Seems happy unless he is riding a horse?

"Don't you think we could ride without being instructed,
    Without any saddle or bridle or spur?
Our legs are so long, and so aptly constructed,
    I'm sure that an accident could not occur.
Let us all of a sudden hop down from the table,
    And hustle downstairs, and each jump on a horse!
Shall we try? Shall we go? Do you think we are able?"
    The Sugar-tongs answered distinctly, "Of course!"

So down the long staircase they hopped in a minute;
    The Sugar-tongs snapped, and the Crackers said "Crack"
The stable was open; the horses were in it;
    Each took out a pony, and jumped on his back.
The Cat, in a fright, scrambled out of the doorway;
    The Mice tumbled out of a bundle of hay;
The brown and white Rats and the black ones from Norway
    Screamed out, "They are taking the horses away!"

The whole of the household was filled with amazement;
    The Cups and the Saucers danced madly about;
The Plates and the Dishes looked out of the casement;
    The Salt-cellar stood on his head with a shout;
The Spoons, with a clatter, looked out of the lattice;
    The Mustard-pot climbed up the gooseberry-pies,
The Soup-ladle peeped through a heap of veal-patties,
    And squeaked with a ladle-like scream of surprise.

The Frying-pan said, "It's an awful delusion!"
    The Tea-kettle hissed, and grew black in the face;
And they all rushed downstairs in the wildest confusion
    To see the great Nutcracker-Sugar-tong race.
And out of the stable, with screamings and laughter
    (Their ponies were cream-coloured, speckled with brown)
The Nutcrackers first, and the Sugar-tongs after,
    Rode all round the yard, and then all around the town.

They rode through the street, and they rode by the station;
    They galloped away to the beautiful shore;
In silence they rode, and "made no observation,"
    Save this, "We will never go back any more!"
And still you might hear, till they rode out of hearing,
    The Sugar-tongs snap, and the Crackers say "Crack!"
Till far in the distance their forms disappearing,
    They faded away; and they never came back!

Lewis Carroll (1832-1898) was not far behind with Alice and her
Wonderland and more nonsense poetry. The work of Lear and Carroll
is atypical of nineteenth century (and earlier) children's verse, which
was moralistic, joyless, and lacking in style. Little of it has survived
the passing of time.

JABBERWOCKY

'Twas brillig, and the slithy toves
    Did gyre and gimble in the wabe;
All mimsy were the borogoves,
    And the mome raths outgrabe.

"Beware the Jabberwock, my son!
    The jaws that bite, the claws that catch!
Beware the Jubjub bird, and shun
    The frumious Bandersnatch!"

He took his vorpal sword in hand:
    Long time the manxome foe he sought—
So rested he by the Tumtum tree,
    And stood awhile in thought.

And as in uffish thought he stood,
    The Jabberwock, with eyes of flame,
Came whiffling through the tulgey wood,
    And burbled as it came!

One, two! One, two! And through and through
    The vorpal blade went snicker-snack!
He left it dead, and with its head
    He went galumphing back.

"And hast thou slain the Jabberwock?
    Come to my arms, my beamish boy!
O frabjous day! Callooh! Callay!"
    He chortled in his joy.

'Twas brillig, and the slithy toves
    Did gyre and gimble in the wabe:
All mimsy were the borogoves,
    And the mome raths outgrabe.

A century after Blake, Robert Louis Stevenson (1850-1894) wrote of the child's real world. *A Child's Garden of Verses* still speaks for childhood, though no longer so loudly and clearly.

FROM A RAILWAY CARRIAGE

Faster than fairies, faster than witches,
Bridges and houses, hedges and ditches;
And charging along like troops in a battle,
All through the meadows the horses and cattle:
All of the sights of the hill and the plain
Fly as thick as driving rain;
And ever again, in the wink of an eye,
Painted stations whistle by.

Here is a child who clambers and scrambles,
All by himself and gathering brambles;
Here is a tramp who stands and gazes;
And there is the green for stringing the daisies!

Here is a cart run away in the road
Lumping along with man and load;
And here is a mill and there is a river;
Each a glimpse and gone for ever!

Contemporary Poems

Twentieth century poetry for children is a widening and deepening field. No longer is there a small "pool" of appropriate subjects for children, nor are there limitations on form. There is a realization that poetry can be for children just as it can be for adults, and that writing down to children or setting up barriers to poems are unnecessary.

Poetry is today. It may not even seem like poetry at first. If one reads Mary Neville's *Woody and Me*, he will see how immediate poetry can be. In natural speech rhythms, the very boyish narrator tells about his life and feelings, for example, "The Morning that Seemed Like Forever"; his part in the program as the space in Merry Christmas; judging whether people prefer children or canaries; and "Art" (Why does it have to be explained?).

It is even better to turn to the children themselves and see what they are saying. *The Real Tin Flower* is the work of one nine-year-old girl, and *Miracles* contains many poems by children.

DEATH

Who set that endless silence
Of her breath?
Death is but death.
Death is like the growing of people
It cannot be stopped.[7]

John Erwin
Age 11
Australia

Contemporary poetry is likely to deal with many forms of reality. *The Ballad of the Burglar of Babylon*, by Elizabeth Bishop, is a long story poem dealing with slums, freedom, crime, and punishment. Lois Lenski's realism in fiction is echoed in her poetry. "Foster Child"[8] is the plea of a child who doesn't care if she's better off now; she wants her real parents. Alley cats and supermarkets are the bases for other poems.

Kay Starbird speaks matter-of-factly of the family, with mother usually pregnant and a none-too-stable father, of the town drunk, and of the gardener with an I.Q. of fifty.

---

[7]Richard Lewis, ed., *Miracles, Poems by Children of the English-Speaking World* (New York: Simon and Schuster, 1966).

[8]Lois Lenski, *The Life I Live, Collected Poems* (New York: Henry Z. Walck, 1965).

It can be particularly exciting to discover the paperbacks, *Little Herder in Spring*[9] and *Little Herder in Summer*,[10] written for the Bureau of Indian Affairs by Ann Nolan Clark. The poems illustrate well the openness of form and content increasingly found in children's poetry.

AFTERNOON

Lying on my back
    under the willows
    I can see an eagle flying
    far above
    in great circles
    against the blue.

I feel
    and see
    and listen,
    but I do not talk.

There is no one to hear me.

There is no one to play with me,
    only the lambs and the baby goats
    and they like each other
    better than me,
    I think.

I am alone.

MEETINGS

For a long time
    there have been meetings
    of many men
    for many days.

At the meetings
    there is talking,
    talking,
    talking.

Some this way.

Some that way.

In the morning
    when my father
    leaves for meeting
    he says to us,

      "When I come here again
      then I will know
      if it is best
      to have many sheep

---

[9]Ann Clark, *Little Herder in Spring* (Washington, D.C.: U. S. Department of Interior, Bureau of Indian Affairs, Branch of Education, n.d.).
[10]Ann Clark, *Little Herder in Summer* (Washington, D.C.: U. S. Department of Interior, Bureau of Indian Affairs, Branch of Education, n.d.).

        or few sheep,
        to use the land
        or let it sleep."

    But
        when my father
        comes home from meeting
        he does not know
        which talking-way to follow.

    Tonight
        when my father
        came home from meeting
        he just sat, looking
        and looking.

    My mother gave him coffee
        and bread and mutton,
        but my father just sat,
        looking.

    Then my mother
        spoke to me.

    She said,
        "A meeting is like rain.

    When there is little talk,
        now and then,
        here and there,
        it is good.

    It makes thoughts grow
        as little rains make corn grow.

    But big talk, too much,
        is like a flood
        taking things of long standing
        before it."

    My mother
        said this to me,
        but I think
        she wanted my father
        to hear it.

The habits and oddities of everyday life—childhood at a more superficial level—are found in many poems for children.

MAGIC

    Magic is to count to ten
        before a car can cross the street
        and honk at you—or mornings when
        you can't let sidewalks touch your feet.

Magic is to jump the cracks—
    to touch whatever's made of blue—
    to cross your fingers with a friend
    who says the same thing you say too.[11]

Myra C. Livingston

Poems for children describe beauty—this one uses both sight and sound:

TREE SONG

O summer tree
Singing to me
A song of shadows blue
Spattered with bright
Trembles of light
Leaves above let through,
When I have made
Of sun and shade
A song of summer too,
Then,
O tree
Singing
to me,
I'll sing my song to you.[12]

Harry Behn

This child's poem shows his feelings:

HURTING

It doesn't hurt no place when I'm sad
I just know I'm sad.[13]

Benny Graves
Age 6
United States

Ideas and sounds are explored in poetry.

FEELINGS ABOUT WORDS

Some words clink
As ice in drink.
Some move with grace:
A dance, a lace.
Some sound thin:
Wail, scream and pin.
Some words are squat:
A mug, a pot,

---

[11]Myra Cohn Livingston, *The Moon and a Star and Other Poems* (New York: Harcourt Brace Jovanovich, Inc., 1965).
[12]Harry Behn, *The Wizard in the Well,* Poems and Pictures by Harry Behn (New York: Harcourt Brace Jovanovich, Inc., 1956).
[13]Lewis, *Miracles.*

And some are plump,
Fat, round and dump.
Some words are light:
Drift, lift and bright.
A few are small:
A, is and all.
And some are thick,
Glue, paste and brick.
Some words are sad:
"I never had . . ."
And others gay:
Joy, spin and play.
Some words are sick:
Stab, scratch and nick.
Some words are hot:
Fire, flame and shot.
Some words are sharp,
Sword, point and carp.
And some alert:
Glint, glance and flirt.
Some words are lazy:
Saunter, hazy.
And some words preen:
Pride, pomp and queen.
Some words are quick,
A jerk, a flick.
Some words are slow:
Lag, stop and grow,
While others poke
As ox with yoke.
Some words can fly—
There's wind, there's high;
And some words cry:
"Goodbye . . .
        Goodbye . . ."[14]

                                    Mary O'Neill

Poetry is a new, imaginative way of seeing.

SKYSCRAPERS

Do skyscrapers ever grow tired
    Of holding themselves up high?
Do they ever shiver on frosty nights
    With their tops against the sky?
Do they feel lonely sometimes
    Because they have grown so tall?
Do they ever wish they could lie right down
    And never get up at all?[15]

                                    Rachel Field

---

[14]Mary O'Neill, *Words, Words, Words*, with decorations by Judy Puissi-Campbell. (Garden City, N.Y.: Doubleday & Co., 1966).
[15]Rachel Field, *Taxis and Toadstools* (Garden City, N.Y.: Doubleday & Co., 1926).

A poem may question one's self-concept.

ROBERT, WHO IS OFTEN A STRANGER TO HIMSELF

> Do you ever look in the looking-glass
> And see a stranger there?
> A child you know and do not know,
> Wearing what you wear?[16]

Gwendolyn Brooks

Of course, there is still verse just for fun.

Poetry is poets who don't set out to write for children, but whose work speaks to them. Robert Frost, William Shakespeare, William Butler Yeats, Dylan Thomas, e. e. cummings, W. S. Gilbert, Edwin Arlington Robinson are just a few who have inadvertently contributed to children's poetry. Among their poems are some that have great meaning and appeal to today's children.

What is poetry? Poetry is a person writing from himself—his experiences, his thoughts, and his feelings, skillfully expressing these through the devices of his craft.

Poetry Is Language.

Poetry is language, using words as tools of communication. The poet does this in very careful and thoughtful ways. The meaning of the word, the sound of the word, its implications, the relationship of that word to other words used, and the totality of the poem all affect his choice of language.

The Language of Carefully Chosen Words: Poets make conscious use of the connotative meanings of words. The dictionary is helpful with the denotative (explicit) meaning, but many words have associations far beyond the specific definition. For example, *The Random House Dictionary of the English Language* cites "a female parent" as the most common meaning of "mother." What does the word "mother" bring to mind? The connotations of a word are those personal ideas and feelings that the statement of that word summons. Mother? warmth, protection, birthday cakes, pink, stories at bedtime? fear, hunger, the inappropriate party dress? What about the words "food," "summer," "hurricane," "Christmas"? The poet who writes about "snow" or "trees" or "summer" suggests far more than scientific realities to the reader.

Rich as a word may be in associations, it must be the right word for the context of the poem. Its meaning must be appropriate to the total poem. Words that express the right shade of meaning for the context, that are explicit rather than general, are part of the poet's art.

---

[16]Gwendolyn Brooks, *Bronzeville Boys and Girls*, Ronni Solbert, illus. (New York: Harper & Row, 1956).

What verbs might one use for the walk of a tired old man who doesn't know where he'll sleep tonight? For a girl who's just been invited to her first dance? For the middle-aged father who is daydreaming on his way to work? What single word best describes the first robin of spring? The shirt that you wish you'd never bought? The food at the picnic? Which word most tellingly describes how the dancer moved: sinuously, gracefully, lightly, airily, joyously? The sun on a cloudy morning: sickly, pale, thin, wan, pallid, dim? The first steps of a young animal: tottered, wobbled, walked, faltered? It depends on precisely what the poet wants to say in the precise context, (and also, of course, how it fits with the rest of what's been said).

The Language of Sound: There are some who say that sound alone makes a poem. This carries to the extreme the generally accepted view that words in poetry are not merely bearers of meaning, but that they should also appeal to the ear. If one were to listen to a poem as he would listen to instrumental music, he could better understand this concept. This enjoyment of sound is the reason that simple verses and poems can be shared with very young children whose language is limited. And it is the reason that some poems attract older children, not because of what the poem has to say, but because the sound of the poem pleases them.

Some words are chosen because their sounds add to their effect. Rustle, bong, punch, sibilant, puff, helter-skelter, slam, gloom, bleat are examples of onomatopoeia. Some poets make up words to suggest what they want to say. In "The Ceremonial Band" (*The Blackbird in the Lilac, Verses for Children*),[17] James Reeves uses "zoomba-zoom" for the heavy sound of the bass, and "pickle-pee" for the light sound of the fife.

Words that sound harsh would not likely be used in a lullaby. Melodious, soothing sounding words would be more suitable, words like "soft," "hush," "sleep," "dream," "sweet and low," and "slumber." In "A Jamboree for J" (*It Doesn't Always Have to Rhyme*), Eve Merriam makes a long list of J words which she thinks all sound joyful. On the other hand, the reader might contrast the words "gloom" and "gaiety." Are the meanings all that distinguish them?

The arrangement of the words helps to make the poem. Meaning, rhythm, effect, and sound all are influenced by the order in which words are placed. Coleridge called for the use of "the best words in the best order."

Appropriately arranged words, chosen for their precision of sound and meaning, words which have the power to evoke personal reactions

[17]James Reeves, *The Blackbird in the Lilac, Verses for Children,* illus. Edward Ardizzone (New York: E. P. Dutton & Co., 1959).

in the reader, are elements with which the poet works. However, he must not be carried away by the words themselves at the cost of their function in the poem. And the poet is sparing in his use of words.

Language that May Be in Rhyme: Poetry may be rhyme. It is most unfortunate that for many people the hallmark of poetry is rhyme. The aural pleasure afforded by words that have identical sounds, and by a structural unity that has a desirable effect are the primary reasons for rhyme. Some writers say the discipline of using rhyme in an honest, meaningful way is a valuable challenge to the writer.

Challenge or albatross? The need to rhyme lessens the poet's opportunities to say what he wants to say. The rhyme may become more important than the content. Many awkward, unnatural poems that don't communicate have resulted from a devotion to rhyming; others are facile and superficial.

Look at poems written by children who have been taught that rhyme and meter are the most important elements of poetry. The results are sad and seem to be no more than a phonetic exercise. Rather than asking himself what he wants to say, the child looks for words rich in rhyming possibilities. (It is interesting to note that the successful creativists are, for the most part, getting unrhymed poetry from children.)

However, many poets can work successfully with rhyme and use it to enhance the totality of the poem. Rhyme offers tremendous possibilities, and people are still inventing ways in which to use it. Rhyme may appear at the ends of lines in varying combinations. For example, Elizabeth Coatsworth, who does work with rhyme, uses the following rhyme schemes in her *Poems*. (Each letter represents a different sound with which to rhyme. *abab* is a poem in which the first and third lines rhyme with each other as do the second and fourth.)

> "January" a b c b d e f e
> "Footprints in the Night" abcd efgd hijk lmnk
> "March" aab ccb
> "It's Raining Still" abcdd efghh ijkll mnopp
> "Song of the Wild Red Strawberries" abcdec fghijh klmnom

Furthermore, rhyme is more than just that which comes at the ends of lines and has the perfection of tree/see, bright/light. Rhyme may be internal, that is, within the line, for example, "And the silken, sad, uncertain rustling of each purple curtain. . . ." Similar sounds may be used inside several lines. In "Strong is the Wind," Coatsworth uses "loud" at the beginning of a line, "boughs" as the second word in the next line, and "resounds" in the middle of the last line of the stanza. The "tittle" in the midst of one line meets the "little" at the end of the following line in Merriam's "Tittle and Jot, Jot and Tittle."

Rhyme may be the combination of sounds that are similar but that are imperfectly matched, for example, rain/again, swallow/yellow, green/stream, shout/crowd, behead/behave. Blake used this kind of end rhyme in "Spring." The similarity may be through vowels (assonance) or consonants (consonance). Repetition of the same consonant at the beginning of words is alliteration. ("Full fathom five thy father lies. . . .")

(There is disagreement as to the extent of the term "rhyme." In *Poetry Handbook; a Dictionary of Terms*,[18] Babette Deutsch includes in her initial definition two major aspects: the repetition of sounds that are the same or similar, and the regularity of intervals at which these sounds occur. And yet she includes alliteration, assonance, and consonance in her definition of rhyme, although these elements are not limited by regularity of occurrence. More useful, perhaps, is Edward Rosenheim's categorizing of all these as aspects of repetition in his *What Happens in Literature; a Guide to Poetry, Drama and Fiction*.[19])

A very obvious example of repetition is that of words or a group of words. Choruses and litanies use repetition. "The House that Jack Built" is an extreme example. Vachel Lindsay repeats a line three times in succession. Others repeat the same line in each stanza of a poem.

One would be on safe ground, then, to say that most poetry has repetition of sound which makes the effect of the poem more pleasurable. The reader may be unaware of the use of this device because the sound is so natural, but a careful analysis is likely to identify aspects of sound repetition.

Poetry Is Experience.

Flora Arnstein suggests in *Poetry in the Elementary Classroom*[20] that every poem is an experience, either imagined or real. This comment may make the whole of poetry more approachable because it should bring poetry to a more personal level. Each of us has experienced and has imagined things he has never done, and this is the stuff of poetry. One can share someone else's experience which will only sometimes be like an experience of his own. Arnstein's point is that through discussions of their similar experiences, children can be led easily into poems.

Poetry draws from the whole of human experience. One of the misconceptions that retards the exploration of poetry is that all poems are

[18]Babette Deutsch, *Poetry Handbook; a Dictionary of Terms* (New York: Grosset & Dunlap, 1957, 1962).

[19]Edward W. Rosenheim, Jr., *What Happens in Literature; a Guide to Poetry, Drama and Fiction* (Chicago: University of Chicago Press, 1960).

[20]Flora Arnstein, *Poetry in the Elementary Classroom*, a publication of the National Council of Teachers of English (New York: Appleton-Century-Crofts, 1962).

about the good, the beautiful, and the feminine. Some are, as they should be, but anything is a fit subject for the poet who feels strongly about it. Browsing through a recent anthology, one finds poems about boats, beggars, a widow bird, the tide, a lone horseman, the wind, a fat lady who goes through life unseeing, the physical and mental discomfort of a Roman soldier, a boxer's "First Fight," witchcraft, madness, death, yearnings on what might have been, "James Honeyman" who invented a deadly gas, a farmer, nonsense, wild geese, a talking candlestick, spring, autumn, gnats, "The Boy Fishing," a call to adventure, the romance of "The Owl and the Pussycat," a child who is deprived and doesn't know it.

Poetry Is Emotion and Thought.

Poetry is feeling. Few poems are just a retelling of an experience. How the poet felt about what happened is intrinsic to most poems, whether he states it directly or whether he implies it. Emotions portrayed in poetry are the range of emotions felt by human beings, although stereotyped views of poetry see it as extremes of happiness or sadness and despair. For many, the intensity of emotion portrayed through poetry is its most distinguishing feature. If one were to reread the poems exemplary of the twentieth century, he would find that all of them reflect the feelings of the writer.

Poetry is certainly thought as well as feeling, cerebral as well as emotional.

Poetry Is Noticing.

A poem is the expression of observation and awareness. In *The Poet's Eye,*[21] Arthur Alexander compares the poet to the scientist in that they are both careful in their observation. The poet notices what many of us miss, and he sees more fully what we see only in broad outline. Not only does he see more comprehensively, but he sees unexpected relationships. Rachel Field's "Skyscrapers" shows this well.

Poetry Is Sensation.

Poetry is imagery, the mental picturing of a reality. Babette Deutsch[22] defines it as the recapturing of "faithful and evocative detail." Smells, pictures, sounds, touch, tastes can all be suggested by the poet's descriptions.

Figures of speech can help evoke images with the help of an observant eye, a creative mind, and an ability to use words. The meta-

---

[21] Arthur Alexander, *The Poet's Eye, An Introduction to Poetry for Young People,* illus. Colleen Browning (Englewood Cliffs, N. J.: Prentice-Hall, 1967).
[22] Deutsch, *Poetry Handbook.*

phor makes a relationship, a comparison between two things not linked in everyday life. Dorothy Aldis sees a fencepost during a snowfall and thinks of marshmallow hats. William D. Sargent calls one of his poems "Wind-Wolves." Elizabeth Madox Roberts' "The Rabbit" has eyes "bursting out of the rim." These all imply far more than they say and spur the reader's imagination.

The simile is more direct and specific, and is introduced by the word "like" or "as." We have many overworked examples of these in everyday speech, for example, "easy as pie," "quick as a wink," "happy as a lark." But great poets have said:

"She walks in beauty like the night. . ." (Byron)

"I saw Eternity the other night like a great ring of pure and endless light." (Henry Vaughan)

Rowena Basten Bennett says that, from high up, "Motor Cars" look like beetles.

Personification gives human attributes to things, placing them in terms of our human lives. It is a form of metaphor.

"The ice gave way and fled." (George Henry Boker)

"The little window where the sun came peeping in at noon. . ."
                                                              (Thomas Hood)

"How troublesome is day." (Thomas Love Peacock)

"The law hath not been dead, though it hath slept." (Shakespeare)

Poetry Is Original.

Poetry is imagination, freshness, the product of a person's creativity. A poem is a unique statement that can be made by only one person. It is written in sincerity and honesty. (These qualities are elusive at best, and the novice has a particularly hard time distinguishing the trite from the original, the sincere from the potboiler, the creative from the superficial.)

Poetry Is Compressed.

Poetry is compact. It crystallizes an experience and does so succinctly. It suggests far more than it says. This is one of the outstanding and unique qualities of poetry. Making every word count, it embodies the essence of what it describes. Through a poem, an aspect of life is made, by the use of words, to come alive for the reader who will interact with the poem and go beyond it. May Swenson's introduction to her *Poems to Solve* is a most compelling explanation of this quality of poetry to encompass far more than it seems to. Poetry often has several levels of meaning. Perhaps in no other characteristic is the relationship between art and poetry so pronounced as in their powers to suggest.

Poetry Is Rhythm.

Rhythm is another of the particularly important features that sets poetry apart. Man is known to be drawn to rhythm, which is an intrinsic part of life. Is this part of a desire for order, form? Whatever it is, we are aware of rhythm and are responsive to it.

Rhythm is a regular, flowing, underlying pulse. It implies movement and evenness. In poetry, rhythm is formalized into meter, which consists of beats and stresses. This is an oversimplified explanation of that which has been made overimportant and overcomplex.

Each line of poetry is made up of a number of syllables and accents. The syllables fall into groups of two or three, with one accent per group (foot). This accent appears at the same place in each foot; it may be the first, second, or third syllable. A line may be made up of any workable number of feet, and the poem made up of lines of the same length.

In actuality, the use of meter is sensible rather than strict. Meter is not a taskmaster that allows no deviation, but rather, a pattern of regularity from which one departs whenever necessary. Meter is like the regularity of our lives, which we frequently vary in such ways as going out to eat, shopping in a nearby town, sleeping late, or taking a vacation. Meter is meat and potatoes; variation from it is the amount of salt and pepper and the knowledge of when to say "No more." There is a great deal of poetry that doesn't use formalized meter but that does use a more spontaneous rhythm.

---

*Poetry Is Form.**

Although much of children's poetry is impossible to categorize according to form, there are some which are classifiable because of certain poetic patterns. A preoccupation with metrics, rhyme schemes, and stanzaic patterns, or the lack of them, overshadows the real stuff of poetry. A recognition, however, of a few of the recurring forms is helpful to anyone approaching poetry. While the ballad, limerick, haiku, tanka, cinquain, free verse, and concrete poetry are not the only forms of children's poetry, they are an important few prevalent in the genre.

A popular form of children's verse is the ballad or folk poem, which is characterized by its presentation of a simple narrative and usually relating a single episode. Since the folk ballad was composed by common folk and was transmitted orally from generation to generation, its origin is uncertain. Campfires, cattle trails, mines, mountains, taverns, and homes provided settings for these verse stories of heroic deeds, love,

---

*This section was written by Marlene Birkman, a postgraduate student in English at Purdue University. Some overlap or variation from the rest of the text has been retained so as to reflect Miss Birkman's overall thoughts on form and to expose the reader to a second viewpoint.

feuds, fairies, ghosts, and domestic happenings. The traditional folk ballad is recognizable by the ballad stanza, usually four lines (the quatrain) with an *abcb* rhyme scheme. Archaic language, repetition, and refrain, which add to the musicality and suspense, and the use of dialogue to develop the action, often appear throughout the stanzas. Except for the refrain, these characteristics are noticeable in the traditional English folk ballad, "Robin Hood and Allan-a-Dale," in which Robin is responsible for bringing about a happy marriage ceremony performed by Little John. It begins:

> Come listen to me, you gallants so free,
>   All you that love mirth for to hear,
> And I will you tell of a bold outlaw
>   That lived in Nottinghamshire.

Of the depressed Allan-a-Dale, whose true love has been kidnapped by the king, Robin inquires:

> "What wilt thou give me," said Robin Hood,
>   "In ready gold or fee,
> To help thee to thy true-love again,
>   And deliver her unto thee?"

It concludes with the summary stanza:

> And thus having ended this merry wedding,
>   The bride lookt as fresh as a queen,
> And so they return'd to the merry green-wood,
>   Amongst the leaves so green.
>   Trad. English

The literary ballad employs the same characteristics as does the folk ballad. The only difference is that its author is known. Although contemporary children's writers seem to have moved from the traditional ballad form to more loosely constructed narrative verse, Rosemary and Stephen Vincent Benet, popular modern literary ballad makers for children, treat in traditional ballad form such unforgettable heroes as Thomas Jefferson, Johnny Appleseed, and Clara Barton in their *A Book of Americans.*

Another form of folk verse is the limerick. Like the ballad, its specific origin remains enigmatic. The limerick supposedly began as a kind of song which was passed around orally. Although there were limericks in print as early as 1821, it was not until Edward Lear published his *Book of Nonsense* in 1846 that they achieved popularity. Children today enjoy the limericks in Lear's *The Complete Nonsense Book* as well as the ones in William Jay Smith's *Typewriter Town* and Sara and John Brewton's *Laughable Limericks.* This favorite form of light verse, often nonsensical, frequently concerns people's actions, manners, and idiosyncrasies. Like the ballad, the limerick follows a definite pattern. It consists of three long rhyming lines (first, second, fifth) and two short rhyming lines (third and fourth). This form is found in "An Old Man from Peru."

There was an old man from Peru   a
Who dreamed he was eating his shoe,   a
He woke in a fright,   b
In the middle of the night   b
And found it was perfectly true.   a

Anon.

Often, limerick makers combine the third and fourth lines, as demonstrated in Lear's limerick about the man with a beard.

There was an Old Man with a beard,
Who said, "It is just as I feared!—
Two Owls and a Hen, four Larks and a Wren,
Have all built their nests in my beard."

Because of its sound-catchiness, its sometimes jumbled and invented words, and its topsy-turvy subject matter, the limerick has proved to be a popular form for children to imitate.

The ancient Japanese form, haiku, or hokku, has become increasingly popular in the United States since World War II. Within the last decade, Harry Behn's *Cricket Songs: Japanese Haiku,* Richard Lewis's *In a Spring Garden,* and Doris Johnson's *A Cloud of Summer, and Other New Haiku*[23] have contributed to its growing popularity among children. Haiku, composed of seventeen syllables, reveals in three lines of five, seven, and five syllables, a single, simple word picture designed to evoke feeling, usually by capturing a moment in nature. In a contemporary haiku, Doris Johnson describes the silence of a snowfall:

Snowflakes fall to earth
lightly as white-kitten-steps.
What sound is so still?[24]

In Japanese haiku, Basho observes a frog jumping in a silent pond. Ransetsu and Onitsura convey their elation over the coming of summer in two haikus about budding wintry twigs and sparrows taking dust baths. Kubonta treats the seasonal in his haiku about a kite that broke away from its string. Not always, however, does this form treat nature or the seasons.

---

[23]Doris Johnson, *A Cloud of Summer, and Other New Haiku,* illus. W. T. Mars (Chicago: Follett Publishing Co., 1967).
[24]From Johnson, *A Cloud of Summer.* Copyright 1967. Reprinted by permission of Follett Publishing Co.

Two relatives of haiku are tanka and cinquain. Tanka, also a Japanese form, is composed of five lines of thirty-one syllables; the first and third lines have five syllables; the second, fourth, and fifth have seven. Virginia Olsen Baron's *The Seasons of Time, Tanka Poetry of Ancient Japan* includes vivid examples of this form. Cinquain, an American counterpart of haiku and tanka, initiated by Adelaide Crapsey, is a five-line, twenty-syllable, unrhymed stanza containing two, four, six, eight, and two syllables. "The Warning," with its single image, is an example of a chilling cinquain.

> Just now,
> Out of the strange
> Still dusk . . . as strange, as still . . .
> A white moth flew. Why am I grown
> So cold?[25]

Unlike the ballad and the limerick, haiku, tanka, and cinquain are not restricted by rhyme patterns. However, because of their prescribed syllabic frameworks, they cannot be classified as free verse.

Ever since the advent of nursery rhymes, most children's poets have been influenced by the regular, rhythmic, rhyming verbal patterns characteristic of this tradition. Poets, bound by a conviction that children's poetry must rhyme, made the poem a restrictive container of feeling. Words, feelings, and experiences, because of contrived rhythm or rhyme, were often reduced to the artificial. Because of such manipulation, many children's poems are feelingless expressions rather than expressions of feeling. Free verse or *vers libre* is an attempt to liberate expression. It is distinguished from conventional poetry forms by its lack of regular rhyme and meter. Unlike ordinary prose, it contains rhythmical units or cadence which the poem's typography often helps suggest. Ann Clark's "Up the Trail" from *Little Herder in Summer*[26] is an example of free verse.

> Morning sunrise sees us climbing
>   up and up
>   on the mountain trail.
>
> There are pine trees
>   standing straight and tall.
>
> Brown pine needles
>   and green grass
>   cover the ground.
>
> Shadows play with the sunlight.
> There is no yellow sand.

---

[25]"The Warning" from *Verse* by Adelaide Crapsey, copyright 1934. Reprinted by permission of Alfred A. Knopf.
[26]Clark, *Herder in Summer.*

> The sheep hurry upward,
>   climbing and pushing
>   in the narrow trail.
>
> I ride after the sheep.
>
> My horse breathes fast.
>
> His feet stumble
>   in the narrow trail.
>
> All day long
>   the sheep climb upward.
>
> They want to eat
>   and I am hungry, too,
>   but my mother says,
>   "No."
>
> All day long we ride
>   to herd the sheep.
>
> Night is almost with us
>   when we reach the top.

In childlike spontaneity, uninhibited by artificial rhymes and rocking chair rhythms, Ann Clark feelingly describes the daylong, sunless experience of following climbing sheep. Although few of her child readers are likely to have had this experience, she invites them to participate by her use of the inclusive "we" and "us." The monotonous, tiring, and depressing climb is felt by the readers through the terse description, identical sentence structures, and the very typography indicative of the "narrow trail." Dorothy Baruch, Hilda Conkling, Carl Sandburg, Langston Hughes, Mary Neville, and Aliki Barnstone have also contributed much to children in the up-dating and up-grading of this genre by loosening the fetters of rhyme.

A most recent form of poetry, existing since 1948 but only having become popular in the fifties, is concrete poetry, which has been successful in the merging of visual, verbal, and auditory elements. More than other poetry forms, concrete poetry relies on the eye; its form is inseparable from its content. Thus, a poem about glass might be found written on glass, a poem about a rock, on a rock. Reinhard Dohl placed his concrete poem about an apple in the shape of an apple.

Like haiku, concrete poetry is beyond paraphrase; each reader brings his thoughts, feelings, and experiences to the discovery of the poem. For example, several carefully selected words may be suspended on a mobile. As the air current moves, the words are juggled and a poem evolves. Two viewers may not see the same word assemblage; perhaps no viewers will agree on the meaning. It is the individual discovery from the visual syntax that is important. Aliki Barnstone introduces a kind of concrete poem to children in *The Real Tin Flower: Poems about the*

World at Nine. "Explanations" defines concretely words such as stairs, speaking, and bowl. It seems likely that the child with his unlimited imagination would be extremely receptive, perhaps more so than adults, to this innovative form.

Much of present day children's poetry lies outside the previously presented forms. Children's poets are occupying a middle ground between writing conventional meters and traditional poetic patterns (rhyming two-line couplets, three-line tercets, or four-line quatrains) and free verse. Poets like Conrad Aiken in *Cats and Bats and Things with Wings*, Mary L. O'Neill in *What Is That Sound?*, and Myra Livingston in *The Moon and a Star and Other Poems* are replacing regular meters with irregular ones, traditional end rhymes with rhymes of all types.

Rigid framework is being discarded for the organic. No longer is poetry appealing only to the ear. Because of unaffected rhythms and rhymes, poets are developing a keener awareness of the poem's graphic design, the appearance of the lines on the printed page. Varied line structure and length of the freer forms attract the eye, making the poem a visual as well as an auditory experience, a design rather than a pattern. Children's poets are seemingly beginning to realize the merits of freedom in form, and consequently, poetry is becoming kinetic. The sight and sound of a poem are becoming natural outgrowths of its purpose, the reflection of a feeling. The result is that the poem is becoming part of, rather than apart from, the child's speech and experience.

Poetry Is a Whole.

Poetry is unity—the bringing together of words, ideas, pictures, feelings, rhythm, and structure into a harmonious whole. There will likely be variety to make the poem more interesting. Poetry is alive and dynamic and today. All the knowledge and humanity of the poet go into giving a poem a sense of vitality.

Poetry Is a Communicator and an Audience.

What is poetry? Poetry is communication, one person writing about something that has meant something to him, reaching out to someone who feels a rapport with what the poet has written. This is far more than the factual communication of the news broadcaster or lecturer, although even these are capable of poetry's communication. It is mind touching mind, heart touching heart. Every poem has an audience somewhere—someone to whom this poem speaks.

A platitude dear to the hearts of librarians is a desire to find "the right book for the right child at the right time." By this same process, a poem communicates when it fits the child as he is at a particular time.

Poetry is a reaction on the part of the reader, not the negative reaction of the person who can't abide even the sight of a poem on the page, but the reaction of a person who has truly listened to a poem. The reaction need not be deep and earth-shaking; it may be one of simple pleasure. A laugh, an appealing mental picture, the relaxation of tension, the security of the familiar poem reread, or the excitement of discovering a new poem by a favorite poet may be the response. We react to the language of poetry, learning the vigor and power of words.

The reader may recognize an experience or a feeling that he has shared. He feels a kinship, a common humanity, perhaps even a sense of relief that he is not alone. The poem may verbalize or at least suggest things that the listener had never been able to put into words. Or it may bring out something that had only been in his subconscious mind. Poetry helps to link us with others, and to know ourselves better. Poetry may help us to gain perspective on our own lives and on life in general. It is a link with the past and with the future.

On the other hand, the reaction may be the stimulation of a new idea or feeling. "That never occurred to me before." "That's absolutely right! Why didn't I think of it?" The effect of this stimulation or insight is likely to go far beyond the initial reaction and could even lead to action.

Poetry may take us beyond what we have experienced or thought and thus extend our being. It can add to the continuous growing and changing that to some extent is a part of all our lives.

A poem may help us appreciate something previously unnoticed or uncared about. A succession of poems that have this effect on us may increase our own awareness and heighten our sensitivities. The boundaries of our personalities are expanded.

As we have more opportunity to feel, we are likely to feel more. This may make life more difficult for the individual, but on the other hand, if there are more people who feel things deeply and care, perhaps ultimately, living will be made less difficult for many.

A poem may stimulate our imagination and creativity. As we see and react to what other people have written, perhaps our own facilities may be strengthened and inspired. Poetry may free us to wonder and to daydream.

Summary.

The writer has heard Myra Cohn Livingston speak of poetry as being both form and force, claiming that, although form is too often the more likely of the two to be stressed, actually force is far more important. Form consists of the formalized devices which the poet uses to give body to his poem—words and rhyme, lines made up of syllables and stresses, the number of each used and where they occur. Form refers to the elements which are concrete and identifiable of which a poem is built.

Force is the total effect of the poem; it reflects the humanity and the skill of the poet—his ability to choose words, to feel, to suggest, to make alive, to communicate. Form is important only insofar as it heightens the impact of the poem. The most important aspect of poetry is its ability to say something to a reader.

Poetry is a human need. Poems have probably existed as long as there has been speech, and rhythm even before that. Poetry possesses something to which man is responsive both as creator and as audience. He could mentally and emotionally exist without poetry, and yet how much he would be missing is immeasurable.

As people begin to realize what poetry really is, they seek out more of it and it is ready whenever the audience is. Poetry is a poet, a poem, a listener, and a rapport among them.

SELECTED REFERENCES

If the reader wants to delve more deeply and technically into poetry as a literary genre, the following list might serve as a good starting point. The recordings are highly recommended, not only because the information they give is understandable and useful, but because they provide poetry readings that make very pleasurable listening. The books, too, approach poetry in a manner that is understandable to a layman.

ALEXANDER, ARTHUR. *The Poet's Eye, An Introduction to Poetry for Young People*. Illustrated by COLLEEN BROWNING. Englewood Cliffs, N.J.: Prentice-Hall, 1967.

DEUTSCH, BABETTE. *Poetry Handbook; A Dictionary of Terms*. New York: Grosset & Dunlap, 1957, 1962.

DREW, ELIZABETH. *Poetry; a Modern Guide to Its Understanding and Enjoyment*. New York: Dell Publishing Co., 1959.

How to Read and Understand Poetry, Educational Audiovisual, Inc. (Pleasantville, New York 10570). Part 1—Poetry: Its Content. Part 2—Poetry: Its Form. (Sound filmstrips with recordings.) Part 3—Interpretation: Reading and Meaning. Part 4—The Interpretation of a Poem (Recordings).

ROSENHEIM, EDWARD W., JR. *What Happens in Literature; a Guide to Poetry, Drama and Fiction*. Chicago: University of Chicago Press, 1960.

Understanding and Appreciation of Poetry, prepared by MORRIS SCHREIBER. Folkway Records FL 9120.

Almost any library will have several books on poetry and, therefore, several viewpoints will be presented. Since poetry is low on science and high on personal reactions, it behooves one to read from as many writers as possible. Differing perspectives, insights, and outright controversy are revealed which serve both to raise questions and to clarify.

There are scores of books written about poetry, some readable to the layman, some not. The following list of books may prove to be of particular help and interest to the novice.

BRIGGS, THOMAS. *Poetry and Its Enjoyment*. New York: Columbia University Press, 1957.

CIARDI, JOHN. *How Does a Poem Mean?* Boston: Houghton Mifflin Co., 1960.

HENSON, CLYDE. *The Gist of Poetics*. New York: Twayne Publishers, 1964.

KORG, JACOB. *The Force of Few Words, an Introduction to Poetry*. New York: Holt, Rinehart & Winston, 1966.

MACLEISH, ARCHIBALD. *Poetry and Experience*. Boston: Houghton Mifflin Co., 1961.

ZILLMAN, LAWRENCE JOHN. *The Art and Craft of Poetry, an Introduction*. New York: Macmillan Co., 1966.

Two books worthy of looking into have a different approach to poetry.

AUSLANDER, JOSEPH, and HILL, FRANK E. *The Winged Horse, The Story of the Poets and Their Poetry*. Garden City, N. Y.: Doubleday & Co., 1955 (1927).

BEHN, HARRY. *Chrysalis; Concerning Children and Poetry*. New York: Harcourt, Brace & World, 1968.

chapter 2

finding poetry

Poetry can contribute to the lives of people only as it is available to them. There is a great wealth of poems for children. If the teacher is going to introduce poetry to children, he must have access to much of this rich supply so that he can find poetry for each child and for many situations. The child should be surrounded with poetry resources from which he can choose freely. There *is* poetry for everyone, but only when the right poem is available at the right time.

Where is poetry found, and in what forms? Poetry resources should be available in the school library/media center, in the public library, and in personal collections. While too many elementary schools still don't have centralized libraries, the range and number of carefully selected resources available in a good media center are vital to an effective poetry program.

Books

Most poetry resources are in print form, although there is a growing collection of related non-print media. Poetry books fall into several definable categories which the user should know.

Anthologies.

The most basic, useful type of poetry book is the general anthology. This brings together poems by many authors and usually provides a good sampling of poetry. Most anthologies group poems by subject. Thus the user can get an overall view of the collection by examining the table of contents. In order to facilitate the location of specific entries, a good anthology has author, title, and subject indexes, and sometimes an index of first lines.

The intended audience may provide some focal point for the anthology. There are books of poetry chosen particularly for girls, or for boys, for the very young child or for the junior high school student, or for the family.

Some anthologists limit their choice of selections to the works of those poets who write specifically for children. Others are concerned with poets whose works, though written for adults, nevertheless are judged to be meaningful to children. Still other anthologists include both. The time element, the era or period in which the poems were written, influences some anthologists; some may choose to emphasize pre-twentieth century poetry, while others may include only the works of modern poets.

Every teacher should have at least one large anthology on his desk. Some school districts furnish this most basic of tools for each teacher, and this seems a custom worthy of nationwide emulation. The only danger in using one good anthology is the tendency to become over-dependent upon it and thus to miss too many of the thousands of other poems to which children might respond. (See Selected References, Part 1-A.)

Some anthologies are more limited in scope and reflect a narrower area than the general anthology. There is a similarity in the organization of both kinds of anthology, the limited and the general. Each has a table of contents indicating the author's choice of poems and their respective categories, and each has an index to aid in the page location of the poems. The majority of the specialized anthologies are tied together by subject, for example, sports, animals, seasons, food. (See Selected References, Part I-B.)

Other anthologies present a type of poem. Haiku, limericks, story poems, and ballads have been gathered into separate collections. (See Selected References, Part I-C.) Still others use country of origin as the common denominator. Recently, books of traditional poetry from various non-Western civilizations have been published. The poems in these books were selected as being particularly suited to children. Our own traditional lore has been collected and published by several folklorists. In recent years, more poems written by children are being published. (See Selected References, Part I-D.)

Books of traditional rhymes of childhood are numerous and essential. A few of these are from our own country, but most of them fit under the Mother Goose umbrella. Mother Goose is simply a term of much-argued origin, and one used to categorize the nursery rhymes that have long been repeated to children.

Illustrations play a far more important part in Mother Goose books than they do in most books of verse. Nursery rhyme books vary in scope from the 800-entry *Oxford Nursery Rhyme Book*, through collections of moderate size, to the single nursery rhyme which, together with verses and illustrations, manages to make up a whole book. (See Selected References, Part I-E.)

All of these anthologies include the work of many poets, but each book is the direct result of the person who chose the poems and brought them together. He may be called the anthologist, the compiler, the editor, or the selector. (In the case of nursery rhyme books, he is probably the illustrator.) He might or might not make remarks of his own, although many collections are enhanced by the anthologist's comments. But he is the creator, through his choice of poems, through his groupings, and through any other effects he uses to present the poetry.

Books by One Author.

The remaining books of poems are those by a single author (occasionally coauthors). These books may or may not have a unifying theme. The style and content of the selections are likely to be more noticeably similar than in anthologies, although the writing of some poets varies tremendously. Anthologies draw from books such as these. (See Selected References, Part I-F.)

In a few cases, a long poem has been interpreted by an illustrator to make a book in itself. (This is comparable to the single nursery rhyme making up a complete book.) Such a volume may be a luxury, rather than a necessity. A few recent poets have told stories in rhyme which have been generously illustrated and published as a single book. (See Selected References, Part I-G.)

Poetry in the Library

To find poetry in a library, the card catalog is always helpful. However, this can be bypassed, and the greater part of a library's poetry collection can be located if one knows that poetry is found in the 800's of the Dewey Decimal Classification. The numbers that are used most often are these:

808.8	General anthologies, subject anthologies.
811	Works by a single American author.
811.08	Anthologies of poems by Americans.
821	Works by a single British author.
821.08	Anthologies of poems by British poets.

Some libraries put all English language poems in the 821 and 821.08 classification for convenience. Folk rhymes may be found in the 398's, and some Mother Goose may be found in the picture book section (under M for Mother Goose or under the illustrator's name). Occasionally, poetry books are classified by subject, for example, Thanksgiving poetry under the number for holidays.

Evaluation Aids — Periodicals

A teacher must evaluate carefully when choosing books of poetry that he will use with his class, whether he plans to purchase the books or to borrow them. There are many poetry books which are excellent, and childhood is too short for children to be subjected to inferior materials.

The easiest way to evaluate children's books (poetry or other) is to accept the judgments of those who are knowledgeable in the area. There is a fairly well-developed fund of literature available to help in selecting books for children. Reviews in magazines aim to evaluate new materials as they are published. Most useful to the person working with elementary school children are:

The Booklist, published by the American Library Association, 50 E. Huron Street, Chicago, Illinois 60611. Subscription $10 per year. Twice a month, September through July and once in August. Semi-annual index in February, annual index in August.

> The sole purpose of this magazine is to evaluate new materials and to suggest the ones that might be suitable for library purchase. Only recommended materials are included. The printed review includes information necessary for ordering and cataloging, and a one-paragraph descriptive annotation. Range of grade levels is suggested. A list, arranged according to author, of recommended children's books is found in the back of each issue.

Bulletin of the Center for Children's Books, published by the University of Chicago Press, 5750 Ellis Ave., Chicago, Illinois 60637 (for the University of Chicago, Graduate Library School). Subscription $6.00 per year. Monthly except August. Annual index in July-August issue.

> The center aims to be a repository for all American books for children published since the Center has been in existence. Because of limited time and personnel, only some of the books received are reviewed in print. Coded symbols ranging from NR (not recommended) to R, with restricted recommendations in some cases, give the value judgment, while the annotations describe and evaluate. One can learn a lot about the practice of book selection from reviews of unacceptable titles. Arrangement is by authors' names. Suggested grade levels are given.

Elementary English, published by the National Council of Teachers of English, 508 S. Sixth Street, Champaign, Illinois 61820. Subscription $10.00 per year. (Part of NCTE membership, Elementary Section.) Monthly, October through May. Annual index in December issue.

> The primary value of *Elementary English* lies in its articles on the teaching of all phases of elementary language arts. "Books for Children"

reviews a relatively small number of books each month. Style and length of reviews vary.

A recent addition to the column is the discussion, or a report, on an interview with an author of children's books. Hopefully, more poets will be included among those who are interviewed. Suggested age ranges are given for each title. Most of the books included are reviewed favorably.

The Horn Book Magazine, published by The Horn Book, Incorporated, 585 Boylston Street, Boston, Mass. 02116. Subscription $6.00 per year. Alternate months, beginning in February. Annual index in December issue.

This publication, completely devoted to literature for youth, is a *must* for anyone involved with children and literature. The articles, news, and reviews are all relevant. The reviews are arranged according to age level (Picture Books, Younger Readers, Older Boys and Girls), and subject (e.g., Poetry, People and Places, Arts and Hobbies). Thus, *The Horn Book Magazine* is the best source for locating poetry easily. The inclusion of a children's book title in the Booklist section indicates a recommendation of that book. There are few adverse criticisms. Books are reviewed and annotated by a regular staff whose names are listed in each issue. The magazine regularly includes poems, particularly those written by children.

School Library Journal, published by R. R. Bowker Co., 1180 Avenue of the Americas, New York, N.Y. 10036. Subscription $7.00 per year. Monthly. (May be subscribed to as part of Library Journal). Annual index in January, bound separately from the issue.

This professional magazine has articles, announcements, and news for the librarian working with children. A good part of each issue is given over to reviews of children's books. The signed reviews are done by people from all parts of the country, although *School Library Journal* staff members do some of the evaluation. This makes for unevenness in reviews, which should be descriptive and critical but which sometimes are only descriptive.

"The Book Review" is divided into five sections—Preschool and Primary Grades, Grades 3-6, Junior High and Up, Reference, and Young Adult. Within each section, the arrangement is alphabetical by author. Both recommended and not recommended materials are included. Entries marked with an asterisk (*) are deemed to be excellent in relation to others of their kind.

Particularly useful are the March and October issues which list titles of books to come. These are arranged by subject. Judging from these lists, there seems to be a trend toward the publication of more poetry books.

In summary, all of these magazines evaluate and annotate new books for children and provide necessary information for the potential purchaser of such books; some of the magazines do even more. The extent to which one uses them depends upon his position and the amount of time he has. The librarian should read all of them faithfully; the teacher may choose one or two to skim through. Both may use the annual indexes to locate evaluations of specific titles.

Evaluation Aids — Comprehensive

Of greater value to the teacher are the comprehensive sources which recommend books. These have aims and organizations similar to the periodicals, but they also have some unique characteristics.

The intent of these sources is to provide a listing of the books one might find in a well-developed media center collection. All the books included are recommended and annotated. By using the indexes and the Dewey numbers, one will find numerous poetry books to consider. (For example, in the 1966 *Children's Catalog* alone, there are forty-three titles listed under the number 821.08.)

The titles included in each source are arranged just as they would be in a library. Author, title, and subject indexes are guides to materials needed. Information for purchasing and cataloging is included, as are suggested grade levels.

GAVER, MARY V., ed. *The Elementary School Library Collection*; a Guide to Books and Other Media, Phases 1-2-3. Newark, N. J.: The Bro-Dart Foundation.

The stated aim is to present high quality material relating to the school's curriculum and to the child's interests. All entries are marked Phase 1, 2, or 3. Phase 1 indicates the most basic titles, suggested for first purchase. As the library grows, and as greater depth in an area is needed, Phases 2 and 3 suggest further titles. This, and the inclusion of nonprint materials, are the particular strengths of *Elementary School Library Collection*.

HODGES, ELIZABETH. *Books for Elementary School Libraries*, An Initial Collection. Compiled and edited by Elizabeth D. Hodges. Chicago: American Library Association, 1969.

The editor, aided by a reactor panel, suggests more than 3,000 titles which she feels would provide a good foundation for a library collection.

SHOR, RACHEL, and FIDELL, ESTELLE A., ed. *Children's Catalog*. New York: The H. W. Wilson Co.

———. *Junior High School Library Catalog*. New York: H. W. Wilson Co.

Children's Catalog aims to provide a list of books which have proven to be useful in work with children, as vouched for by experienced librarians and specialists in children's literature. A hardcover edition appears every five years and is supplemented by annual paperbacks. Each hardcover edition fully replaces previous publications.

Anyone working with older elementary children might also want to use the *Junior High School Library Catalog*, which first appeared in 1965.

Evaluating Poems

One who wants to become acquainted with the field of children's poetry might start by using at least some of the aforementioned sources (and, it is hoped, this book). Personal recommendations from the knowledgeable are helpful. Browsing through and reading from generally well-accepted poetry books helps to develop standards by which to judge poems. Few poetry books are intended to be read in consecutive order from cover to cover; rather, they are to be sampled.

It is advisable that one train himself to listen to poems with his inner ear and picture them with his inward eye (favorite expressions of the poets!) Before long, he will become aware of individual poets, of poems that are found over and over, of style, of subjects explored by poets, and by his own response to various poems. One might also train himself to observe the physical aspects of a poetry book, its organization. With this increasing background, he can begin to branch out and make his own evaluations of poems and books.

Perhaps the idea of leaning heavily on the judgments of others is difficult to accept. Experience with newcomers to the field of children's literature has shown that simply plunging into poetry without guidance is often self-defeating; that more time is spent than taste developed. Over the years, there are things about poetry and poets that knowledgeable people have agreed upon, and one would be wise to start from here.

The general feeling is that exposure to good poetry will make the inferior poetry unacceptable. Unfortunately, this is only an article of faith. Meaningful guidance from a wise and understanding teacher, whether encountered in person or through his writing, should help to develop discrimination in poetry.

On the other hand, there are many who feel that thoughtful exposure to a great quantity of poetry, regardless of merit, will lead one to recognize and appreciate quality. Perhaps for the reader this will be the preferred approach.

Whatever the method, deductive or inductive, it is agreed that one can only learn how to evaluate and select poetry by getting to know poems. When one has felt the rhythm of free-flowing poetry, sing-song verses lose their appeal. After the powerful expression of such poets as Shakespeare, Teasdale, and de la Mare, the merely cute becomes recognizable as such. The power of poems like Blake's "The Tyger" and Hughes' "Black Like Me" causes one to look askance at didactic poems. Honest expressions of emotion, naturally stated, help one realize that convoluted, superficial poetry is insufficient and unnecessary.

In choosing books of poetry to use with children, the teacher may be choosing those he wants to purchase or those he wants to borrow. Certainly, content and approach, as well as quality, will help determine the choice. The group with whom he will use these books is a basic factor in selection. Unfortunately, the selection process is not reduceable to formula. However, some general suggestions may be made in evaluating and selecting books of poetry.

Evaluation of Poetry Books

Evaluation is the process of using criteria to help determine quality.

SUGGESTED EVALUATION OF BOOKS OF POETRY FOR CHILDREN

OVERALL SELECTION OF POEMS

> Consistent quality
> Relate well to each other, whether through contrast, variety, scope, or similarity
> Relate well to purpose of editor or poet
> Inclusiveness (scope)
>> Poet(s) included
>> Sampling, variety of poetry
>> Number of poems
>> Subjects
>> Types of poems
> Useful organization
>> Arrangement
>> Keys to the arrangement
>>> Table of Contents
>>> Indexes

INDIVIDUAL POEM

DESIRABLE	UNDESIRABLE
1. Childlike, that is, it seems to come from and/or relate to a child's world.	1. Poem about children rather than for them; too far away from their experience and interest to have any appeal.
2. Quality compares favorably with that of poems generally considered good; use of rhythm; honesty of emotion; use of language; overall effect; vividness of imagery.	2. Quality compares unfavorably with that of poems generally considered good; overly rhythmic to the point of being singsongy; supersentimental or saccharine; unnatural, affected; unimaginative use of words.
3. Understandable to children; capable of helping them stretch their imaginations and understanding.	3. Too difficult or too simple.
4. Fresh and original, even if it is a subject familiar to poetry.	4. Hackneyed, merely "cute"; didactic.
5. Respectful of the child as a person.	5. Condescending, oversimplified.

(See also criteria in Chapter 3, pages 69 and 70.)

FORMAT
    Illustrations
        Enhance the text
        Give additional dimension
        Capture the spirit of the book
        Are suggestive rather than restrictive
        Appropriate medium, technique, color
        Good art
    High quality paper of an appropriate color
    Print
        Appropriate size for intended reader
        Readable
    Page layouts
        Uncluttered
        Desirable relationship of print to white space
    Dimensions of book: appropriate to content
    Cover (While a sturdy, attractive cover is an asset, the use of plastic jackets and/or reinforced bindings makes this a less important criterion.)

Selection of Poetry Books

In selection, one tries to set up a somewhat representative collection of materials in light of potential users, refining this collection in terms of actual usage and the availability of new materials.

GUIDELINES	IMPLICATIONS
1. Selection rests on a belief in evaluation, that what we choose for our purposes has been rated as desirable by people in a position to judge.	1. Reputable printed evaluation sources have recommended any book considered. Or, the reader or other competent professionals have reviewed it and evaluated it favorably.
2. Selection is for a particular group of children at a particular place in space and time. One chooses for people, not for an abstract, ideal collection.	2. One should get to know the larger community, the school and the specific group for whom he selects, being aware particularly of the capabilities, needs, and interests of group members.
3. Selection must take into consideration the scope of poetry and poetry materials for children, and aim to reflect the genre.	3. Included should be all kinds of books, many poets (both those who write specifically for children and those whose adult

poems are useful with children), traditional and modern poetry, non-book poetry materials, varied approaches to poetry, and forms of poetry.

4. A collection is an entity, not just a lot of materials haphazardly chosen. Materials are chosen in relation to what is already available. A foundation collection may first be established, and then gradually be built up by additions.

4. Initially, the reader will probably rely primarily on large anthologies. He will study relationships of titles. Is more depth and breadth needed? Are significant poets missing? Does the material being considered complement or supplement the collection? Where else in the community are materials available? What effect will the holdings of that agency have on the reader's selection?

5. Actual usage helps determine selection. While a good collection has a wide scope (#3), depth is determined by what people want.

5. It is advisable to duplicate titles as needed and to purchase heavily in the areas which are particularly popular.

6. Content, rather than copyright date or price, should determine suitability. For children, a new book is one that is shiny and clean, or even just unfamiliar.

6. It is also advisable to select recently published books, as well as those written in times past, if they seem appropriate and suitable. Concrete poetry and Blake both ought to be considered seriously. There is no rush to get the latest in poetry books; it is best to wait for reviews or a chance to examine new titles.

Ideally, evaluation and selection for the media center will be done by the professional librarian (media specialist), assisted by teachers.*

The school and/or public library should provide constantly changing collections of books for the group, books chosen by the teacher, the librarian, and the children. In addition to these resources, the teacher will want to develop his own smaller collection of poetry books.

---

*Note: The series editor would state "along with" rather than "assisted by." The author's phrase has been left unchanged, however. This is an issue which, perhaps, should be discussed in a class.

Poetry in New Formats

Increasingly, producers of non-print materials are finding opportunities to package poetry. Is this opportunity or sacrilege? Is it appropriate to present poetry through films, filmstrips, transparencies, slides,
recordings, picture sets, objects, kits of materials? Do such approaches
deny the essence of poetry? Do they prevent the child from imagining
and interpreting for himself what the poet is saying? Or are audiovisual
materials the best way to reach today's electronically oriented children?

Although this question can be discussed philosophically, one would
do better to see what is available and then make the decision as to
whether or not to use poetry in new formats. At best, non-print media
can add new dimensions and interest to poetry. At worst, they tend to
dull the imagination and taste.

First, where will non-print media be found? Modern libraries accept
the multimedia approach to learning and should include poetry in more
than just print format. District media centers back up these collections
(or sometimes try to compensate for a lack of central libraries). The
reader will find that there are state agencies that circulate materials.
It may be well to consider using the materials that are found in college
and university libraries, particularly at the schools where there is a
curriculum in teacher education. Films may be rented from several
sources.

Evaluating and Selecting Poetry in Non-Print Form

The reader may be preparing to start a local collection of non-print
poetry media. Whether borrowing or buying, he would be wise to
preview and evaluate all materials under consideration. Most producers
will send copies of their materials for preview to those who are seriously
considering purchase.

Unfortunately, there is little published professional evaluation of
non-book material. Such evaluations could serve to help screen materials
so that one would need to preview only those that sounded as if they
were possibilities. A few reviews will be found in *Horn Book. The Booklist* and *School Library Journal* now have columns in each issue devoted
to the evaluation of non-print media, and this coverage is likely to
increase. *Elementary School Library Collection* includes records, filmstrips, transparencies, and picture sets. (Other sources that include an
evaluation are found in Part II-A of the Selected References. Part
II-B lists unevaluated titles that the reader might want to preview.)

Once a specific material is in hand, the teacher is ready to begin
evaluation. For general criteria, audiovisual textbooks may be consulted.
(See Part II-C of the Selected References.)

The following specific criteria for poetry in non-print format is suggested:

1. Is the subject worth doing?
2. Does this new format retain the spirit of the poem(s) used?
   Appropriate vocal interpretation: voice(s) used; approach; style of reading?
   Appropriate visual interpretation: medium; color; size; style?
3. Is it a gimmick, or an enrichment, going beyond what could be done by the leader and the children?
4. Could this be an avenue into poetry for the child with little interest in the genre?
5. Does it do all the work for the child, or is his imagination stimulated? For the child who gets his poetry only through non-print media, does this example help him to build a true concept of poetry?
6. Does it contribute to an understanding of and an interest in poetry? (That which merely entertains is to be avoided.)
7. Does it have vitality? It may be technically and aesthetically impeccable, but deadly. Are children likely to respond to it?
8. How would the reader use it? The more opportunities one sees for utilization, the more desirable it seems.

Application of Criteria.

Perhaps some examples will help illustrate these criteria.

A teacher, using two screens, a tape recorder, overhead and slide projectors, gives a class a seven minute exposition on haiku. Leaving out the practical considerations of coordinating such a sophisticated production (technology and auxiliary aides will eventually take care of that), the fact remains that the simplicity of haiku is lost in a wealth of gadgetry. The presentation tells quickly and matter-of-factly what haiku is. The teacher could better read from the book or present the filmstrip, *In a Spring Garden,* and ask a few thoughtful questions about the kind of poetry he has presented.

A poet reads his choice of his own poetry. The voice has its limitations, but this is the real person, and hearing his voice adds a link to our feeling for him. We tend to read more of his poetry after hearing him and we can almost hear his voice reading it to us. His oral interpretation of poems reveals new meanings.

An actress reads poetry for the very young as she would do a serious dramatic reading for adults. The diction and interpretation are well done, but the reading lacks any sense of warmth and involvement, or awareness of the would-be audience.

A set of pictures is packaged to accompany an album of poetry. The idea seems to be to give the child something to look at while he listens. (If this is a valid idea, two hours spent going through old magazines would be likely to yield pictures just as useful.)

A slide set, accompanied by taped musical background and the reading of wind poems, has a shimmering, windy quality. The illustrations are original, and the photography highlights the medium used. The visual, verbal, and musical fit together well and heighten interest. Adults who see the set react to it by wanting to create something like it. (See Selected References, Part II-D for a list of recommended poetry materials in audio and/or visual form.)

The entry of the paperback into the field of children's poetry provides an inexpensive way in which to build personal and classroom collections. Selective lists of paperbacks are now available. For up-to-date listings, a check in *Paperbound Books in Print* will indicate the availability in soft cover of a given title.

Other Sources of Poetry

Poetry is not limited to books and to audiovisual materials classified accordingly. The reader will want to investigate in the media center other materials that are poetic in nature, and then develop a list of such materials. He may wish to copy from these books poetic sentences or paragraphs that he might like to share sometime.

Books and reproductions of music and art are closely related to poetry, sharing rhythm, crystalization of experience and emotional origins. Many music books have settings for poems that the reader might want to use.

Folklore and poetry are close, sometimes to the point that they are one and the same. Man early began telling of his deeds and those of his tribe; he accompanied his work with words. Later he told and sang of heroes and love and treachery and fools and the common people in uncommon situations. Some of these works remain with us, both as prose and as poetry. Even the prose retains some qualities of poetry, particularly the feeling for the right word and the smoothing away of unnecessary words.

Occasionally, a biographer will react to his subject in such a way that the resultant style is often poetry, for example, Sandburg's *Abe Lincoln Grows Up*.[1]

Books of religion, of the type acceptable in school libraries, have statements of faith of divergent peoples, often so stated that one would want to share them with children, such as *God Is in the Mountain*.[2]

---

[1]Carl Sandburg, *Abe Lincoln Grows Up* (New York: Harcourt, Brace & World, 1928).
[2]Ezra Jack Keats, *God Is in the Mountain* (New York: Holt, Rinehart & Winston, 1965).

Books of information tend to be very hardheaded, and yet, one may discover a gem which combines facts and poetic style, for example, Behn's *All Kinds of Time*.[3]

In fiction and picture books, one can discover some wonderful evocative writing. These books may be more appreciated by those who know and love poetry. An example of this type is *The Bat Poet*.[4]

Magazines and newspapers often print poetry. While much of it is sleazy or slick, there are some poems worth clipping or copying. Children's and teachers' magazines are full of potboilers that are demeaning to the genre and to children. And yet, the same magazines may include fine examples of poetry by children.

Two good sources for children's poems are *The Horn Book* (its poetry by adults is also excellent) and the annual October issue of the *Elementary School Journal*, published by the University of Chicago.

Teachers would be wise to save the poems that their pupils have written, that is, if the children are willing to let them keep copies. It is also advisable to listen to what children say and write it down; often their speech is unconsciously poetic.

A file of poetry continually being built up is a necessity. Successful teachers copy poems that appeal to them. Books of poems for adults, and books that are generally unacceptable often yield single poems useful to the teacher. It is advisable to be alert for pictures, music, films, records, films, and filmstrips that might be used as part of the poetry program.

Summary.

There is a large and growing collection of poetry materials for children. If poetry is to have any impact, it must be readily available to children and to those working with them. Poems that are attractive, that are varied in content, difficulty, and approach, that are carefully chosen for quality and appeal, that are appropriate to the group, and that are not limited by form or personal prejudice, providing something of interest and potential effect for everyone, can be found among these materials.

The teacher develops his acquaintance with poetry through use of professional tools and through wide previewing of materials. His aims are to develop discrimination and appreciation, to get to know poems and the packages in which they come, and to know sources from which to get materials. From this knowledge is built up a collection of poetry for the personal and group enjoyment of students and teachers.

But just knowing professional aids and the assimilation of standards for judging poetry are insufficient. Awareness of poetry in the world in

---

[3]Harry Behn, *All Kinds of Time* (New York: Harcourt, Brace & World, 1950).
[4]Randall Jarrell, *The Bat Poet*. Pictures by Maurice Sendak (New York: Macmillan Co., 1964).

general, the willingness to organize usable files in which to accumulate one's discoveries round out the process of building poetry collections. Most important is the careful selection of materials which are plentiful in number and instantly accessible to all.

SELECTED REFERENCES

I. Books of Poetry

  A. General Anthologies

Anthologies tend to rely on the tried and true rather than on recent poetry or works of adult poets worthy of consideration for children. Some are excellent in their universality of selection, others predictable. Since anthologies are the most economical vehicle for poems, care must be taken to get as broad and interesting a selection as possible.

ADSHEAD, GLADYS, and DUFF, ANNIS, comps. *Inheritance of Poetry.* With decorations by NORA S. UNWIN. Boston: Houghton Mifflin Co., 1948.

A collection with great respect for children; has selections from over 2,000 years. Especially fine for a family to own. No table of contents, although there is a subject arrangement. Indexes include one of musical settings.

ARBUTHNOT, MAY HILL, and ROOT, SHELTON L., JR. *Time for Poetry.* 3d ed. Illustrated by ARTHUR PAUL. Chicago: Scott, Foresman & Co., 1967.

A large collection of poetry, aiming to be representative. The contents tend to the often-included, making it a basic although "safe" collection. There is a large and helpful section called "Keeping Children and Poetry Together." No other anthology serves so well the adult working in education.

Association for Childhood Education. *Sung Under the Silver Umbrella,* Poems for Young Children. Illustrated by DOROTHY LATHROP. New York: Macmillan Co., 1939.

One of the small group of anthologies with poems particularly selected for the very young. Unfortunately, the format is rather dated. The foreword by Padraic Colum is a *must.*

BLISHEN, EDWARD, comp. *Oxford Book of Poetry for Children.* With illustrations by BRIAN WILDSMITH. New York: Franklin Watts, 1963.

The most attractive-looking anthology to date, with the bright illustrations of Brian Wildsmith. Heavy on English poets and older works; many of the poems are not found elsewhere.

BOGAN, LOUISE, and SMITH, WILLIAM JAY. *The Golden Journey,* Poems for Young People. Chicago: Reilly & Lee Co., 1965.

Some poems will help children expand their interest in poetry; others will introduce them to poetry they may have missed earlier. Wide range of usefulness and appeal.

CLARK, LEONARD, comp. *Drums and Trumpets,* Poetry for the Youngest. Illustrated by HEATHER COPLEY. Chester Springs, Pa.: Dufour Editions, 1962.

Chosen for the adult to read to the young child who is being introduced to poetry. Introduction contains valuable philosophy and guidance of the compiler. Some of the selections are new to anthologies. The collection is very English, heavy on de la Mare and Andrew Young. The illustrations, although modest, should add a quiet interest for the young listener.

CLITHERO, SALLY, comp. *Beginning-to-Read Poetry,* Selected from Original Sources. Illustrated by ERIK BLEGVAD. Chicago: Follett Publishing Co., 1967.

Not as limited as the title suggests. A small, pleasant collection of short poems of immediate interest to a young child.

DE LA MARE, WALTER JOHN. *Come Hither,* A Collection of Rhymes and Poems for the Young of All Ages. Decorations by Warren Chappell. New York: Alfred A. Knopf, 1957.

A rich collection of almost 500 poems. De la Mare's introduction tells of his own introduction to poetry, as well as "The Story of This Book." A lengthy section at the end, "About and Roundabout," has notes and comments on many of the poems in the book. Greatest use will be by the adult with the child, as the format is rather discouraging.

———. *Tom Tiddler's Ground,* A Book of Poetry for Children. Chosen and annotated by WALTER DE LA MARE. Foreword by LEONARD CLARK, and drawings by MARGERY GILL. New York: Alfred A. Knopf, 1962.

Resulting from the success of *Come Hither,* this anthology is for a more limited group of young children. Poems are not arranged in sections, but rather, in a sort of continuum, with one poem leading naturally into the next. More attractive than *Come Hither,* it also has a section of de la Mare's comments.

DUNNING, STEPHEN; LUEDERS, EDWARD; and SMITH, HUGH, comps. *Reflections on a Gift of Watermelon Pickle and Other Modern Verse.* Designed by DONALD MARVINE. New York: Lothrop, Lee & Shepard Co., 1967.

Modern poetry chosen for modern young people and illustrated with equally modern photographs.

FERRIS, HELEN, ed. *Favorite Poems Old and New.* Illustrated by LEONARD WEISGARD. Garden City, N.Y.: Doubleday & Co., 1957.

Almost a source book; there are 700 poems in this volume.

GEISMER, BARBARA PECK, and SUTER, ANTOINETTE BROWN. *Very Young Verses.* Illustrated by MILDRED BRONSON. Boston: Houghton Mifflin Co., 1945.

Short, simple rhymes, mostly of the child's world. Included are many "verses no child should miss." There are too few collections for children this young, but there is danger in restricting children to this level.

HANNUM, SARA, and REED, GWENDOLYN E., comps. *Lean Out of the Window,* An Anthology of Modern Poetry. Decorations by RAGNA TISCHLER. New York: Atheneum Publishers, 1965.

Modern poetry for the more mature child. Useful as an introduction to modern writers and styles.

HUBER, MIRIAM BLANTON. *Story and Verse for Children.* 3d ed. New York: Macmillan Co., 1965.

The selections are familiar, with no recent poets. A comfortable, but not stimulating collection.

IRESON, BARBARA, ed. *The Barnes Book of Nursery Verse.* Illustrated by GEORGE ADAMSON. New York: A. S. Barnes & Co., 1960.

Chosen for the child up to age seven, this very large collection offers perhaps the widest choice for this age level. Heavy on traditional verse.

LARRICK, NANCY, comp. *Piper, Pipe That Song Again!* Poems for Boys and Girls. Illustrated by KELLY OECHSLI. New York: Random House, 1965.

A good size — large enough for variety but not overpowering. Authors, poems tend to the familiar, although not as much so as *The First Book of Poetry.* One poem leads naturally into another.

LIVINGSTON, MYRA, ed. *A Tune Beyond Us,* A Collection of Poetry. Illustrated by JAMES J. SPANFELLER. New York: Harcourt, Brace & World, 1968.

Modern selections reaching into space and time. Almost entirely "adult" poetry, it challenges the reader. The quantity of unfamiliar poems is refreshing.

McEWEN, CATHERINE SCHAEFER, comp. *Away We Go,* 100 Poems for the Very Young. Illustrated by BARBARA COONEY. New York: Thomas Y. Crowell Co., 1956.

Very simple, short poems of everyday life.

NASH, OGDEN. *Everybody Ought to Know.* Verses selected and introduced by Ogden Nash. Illustrated by ROSE SHIRVANIAN. Philadelphia: J. B. Lippincott Co., 1961.

This poet's selection of poems that everyone should have heard.

PETERSON, ISABEL, ed. *The First Book of Poetry.* Illustrated by KATHLEEN ELGIN. New York: Franklin Watts, 1954.

Not as elementary as the title suggests, this serves as an excellent, although not up-to-date, introduction to children's poets and poems of established appeal. For the adult new to children's poetry, this could be a good first book.

READ, HERBERT, ed. *This Way, Delight,* A Book of Poetry for the Young. Illustrated by JULIET KEPES. New York: Pantheon Books, 1956.

Read's purpose is to introduce the delight of poetry, through works of poets who have spoken to children from as far back as the fifteenth century up to the present. At the end of the book, there is an excellent chapter on poetry.

SECHRIST, ELIZABETH, ed. *One Thousand Poems for Children*; based on the selections of Roger Ingpen. With decorative drawings by HENRY C. PITZ. Philadelphia: Macrae Smith Co., 1946.

An excellent source book because of its size, but it is very weak on modern poets.

SMITH, JANET ADAM. *The Looking Glass Book of Verse.* Illustrated by CONSUELO JOERNS. New York: Random House, 1959.

The compiler chose these poems for eight-to-fourteen-year-olds, feeling that, at that age level, children take more delight in poetry than they ever will again. She aims for variety in mood and tone and covers a particularly wide range of subjects.

SMITH, JOHN, comp. *My Kind of Verse.* Decorations by URI SHULE-VITZ. New York: Macmillan Co., 1968.

The scope of this collection, selected largely from adult poetry, is indicated by the Table of Contents: Songs and Simples — Magic and Mystery — Tall Tales — Odd Bods — Places, Weathers, Creatures, Things — Stuff and Nonsense — Wisdoms, Praise, Prayers, and Graces.

THOMPSON, BLANCHE JENNINGS, ed. *All the Silver Pennies* (Combining *Silver Pennies* and *More Silver Pennies*). Decorations by URSULA ARNDT. New York: Macmillan Co., 1967.

Some poems not often found are included in this selection. Thompson's comments before each poem sometimes provide helpful information and stimulation. Too often, the comments are patronizing in tone and didactic in nature.

UNTERMEYER, LOUIS, ed. *Rainbow in the Sky.* Illustrated by REGINALD BIRCH. New York: Harcourt, Brace & World, 1935.

A favorite—a large collection with lots of variety in a rather attractive format. Untermeyer's brief comments at the beginning of each section are both enjoyable and useful. The lack of contemporary poets is a definite limitation.

——. *The Golden Treasury of Poetry.* Selected and with a commentary by LOUIS UNTERMEYER. Illustrated by JOAN WALSH ANGLUND. New York: Golden Press, 1959.

——. *The Magic Circle,* Stories and People in Poetry. Illustrated by BETH and JOE KRUSH, New York: Harcourt, Brace & World, 1952.

B. Anthologies — Single Subject

ADOFF, ARNOLD, ed. *I Am the Darker Brother,* An Anthology of Modern Poems by Negro Americans. Drawings by BENNY ANDREWS. New York: Macmillan Co., 1968.

Modern poems by Negro Americans — stark, frank, moving. Includes work of Langston Hughes, Gwendolyn Brooks, Leroi Jones, Claud McKay, Richard Wright, Countee Cullen, Robert Hayden.

AGREE, ROSE, ed. *How to Eat a Poem and Other Morsels,* Food Poems for Children. Illustrated by PEGGY WILSON. New York: Pantheon Books, 1967.

Eve Merriam's advice on biting into poetry begins this collection of poems about food.

BRAMBLETT, ELLA. *Shoots of Green,* Poems for Young Gardeners. Illustrated by INGRID FETZ. New York: Thomas Y. Crowell, 1968.

Spring, planting, vegetables, garden animals, pushcarts and florists, seeds, autumn.

BREWTON, SARA and JOHN E. *America Forever New,* A Book of Poems. Drawings by ANN GRIFALCONI. New York: Thomas Y. Crowell, 1968.

Quite a large selection, concerned with America historically, sociologically, physically, and presently.

———. *Bridled with Rainbows,* Poems About Many Things of Earth and Sky. Decorations by VERA BOCK. New York: Macmillan Co., 1950.

School, travel, clothing, play, the city and the country, weather, the sky, the sea, and holidays are headings for groups of poems. To be used as a complement to the Brewtons' *Under the Tent of Sky* and *Gaily We Parade.*

———. *Birthday Candles Burning Bright,* A Treasury of Birthday Poetry. Decorations by VERA BOCK. New York: Macmillan Co., 1960.

———. *Christmas Bells Are Ringing,* A Treasury of Christmas Poetry. Illustrated by DECIE MERWIN. New York: Macmillan Co., 1951.

Gifts, decorations, Santa Claus, the excitement of Christmas, the time after Christmas, all are included, as well as poems about the first Christmas.

———. *Gaily We Parade,* A Collection of Poems About People, Here, There and Everywhere. Illustrations by ROBERT LAWSON. New York: Macmillan Co., 1964.

———. *Under the Tent of Sky,* A Collection of Poems About Animals Large and Small. With Drawings by ROBERT LAWSON. New York: Macmillan Co., 1937.

COLE, WILLIAM, comp. *Beastly Boys and Ghastly Girls.* Drawings by TOMI UNGERER. Cleveland: World Publishing Co., 1964.

An antidote to those who shun poetry as "sissy stuff" — young villains of all shades are described in verse.

——. *The Birds and the Beasts Were There*, Animal Poems Selected by WILLIAM COLE. Woodcuts by HELEN SIEGL. Cleveland: World Publishing Co., 1963.

A hefty collection of animals grouped by similarities and distinguished by variety.

——. *Humorous Poetry for Children.* Illustrated by ERVINE METZL. Cleveland: World Publishing Co., 1955.

An excellent introduction suggests that reading this kind of poetry is "a way of approaching serious poetry sideways." Alphabetically arranged by poets' names. Not only Lear, but A. E. Housman, Ogden Nash, John Keats, T. S. Eliot, and many others.

——. *I Went to the Animal Fair.* Illustrated by COLETTE ROSSELLI. Cleveland: World Publishing Co., 1958.

Some classic animal poems and some less well-known ones in a simple collection for the younger reader/listener's enjoyment.

——. *Oh, What Nonsense!* Drawings by TOMI UNGERER. New York: Viking Press, 1966.

An uncluttered book, with amusing illustrations to complement the zany poetry.

——. *Poems for Seasons and Celebrations.* Illustrated by JOHANNES TROYER. Cleveland: World Publishing Co., 1961.

A delightful collection of poems new and old, serious and humorous. Twenty-six seasons and holidays are celebrated.

——. *Poems of Magic and Spells.* Illustrated by PEGGY BACON. Cleveland: World Publishing Co., 1960.

Strange happenings, granted wishes, mermen, witches, ghosts, hauntings. Moods vary from lighthearted to somber.

——. *The Sea, Ships and Sailors,* Poems, Songs and Shanties Selected by WILLIAM COLE. With drawings by ROBIN JACQUES. New York: Viking Press, 1967.

A lusty, rollicking collection — from buccaneers to the bottom of the sea, from moods to merry stories. Poems tend to be long and are often touched with humor.

EATON, ANNE THAXTER. *Welcome Christmas!* A Garland of Poems. Decorated by Valenti Angelo. New York: Viking Press, 1955.

Virtually all the selections, though non-denominational, relate to the first Christmas. Thus the feeling is quiet and spiritual. Many animal poems.

HAZELTINE, ALICE, and SMITH, ELVA S., comps. *The Year Around,* Poems for Children. Decorations by PAULA HUTCHISON. Nashville: Abingdon Press, 1956.

Arranged by season, and within that, by month or holiday. There is always a need for seasonal poetry.

HOWARD, CORALIE, comp. *The First Book of Short Verse.* Illustrated by MAMORU FUNAI. New York: Franklin Watts, 1964.

Much more exciting than the title implies. Poems from many sources, including children. Italicized comments and questions throughout the book can heighten appreciation.

LARRICK, NANCY, sel. *On City Streets,* An Anthology of Poetry. Illustrated with photographs by DAVID SAGARIN. New York: M. Evans & Co., and distributed in association with J. B. Lippincott Co. (Philadelphia), 1968.

A wide variety of poems, mostly by twentieth century poets. The choice is fresh and timely; more than 100 children living in cities helped in the selection process. The grim reality of a city — poverty, alienation, disillusionment — is vividly portrayed, as are some lighthearted, humorous views of the city.

LOVE, KATHERINE, comp. *A Little Laughter.* Illustrations by WALTER H. LORRAINE. New York: Thomas Y. Crowell Co., 1957.

For somewhat younger children than the ones for whom Cole's *Humorous Poetry* was compiled. Fun for all, and particularly useful for the reluctant ones.

MACDONALD, GERALD D. *A Way of Knowing,* A Collection of Poems for Boys. Illustrated by CLARE and JOHN ROSS. New York: Thomas Y. Crowell Co., 1959.

Works encompassing many centuries and styles; should help disprove the notion that poetry is not for boys. Many selections are those not so often found in anthologies.

MORRISON, LILLIAN. *Sprints and Distances,* Sports in Poetry and the Poetry in Sport. Illustrations by CLARE and JOHN ROSS. New York: Thomas Y. Crowell Co., 1965.

It's a revelation that there is so much exciting poetry relating to sports. This should be a wonderful source for people who look askance at poetry or sports.

PLOTZ, HELEN, comp. *Imagination's Other Place,* Poems of Science and Mathematics. Illustrated with wood engravings by CLARE LEIGHTON. New York: Thomas Y. Crowell Co., 1955.

The compiler sees many relationships between science and poetry —sense of wonder, need to communicate, order. Arranged according to subject field, with a section on men of science.

———. *Untune the Sky,* Poems of Music and the Dance. Illustrated with wood engravings by CLARE LEIGHTON. New York: Thomas Y. Crowell Co., 1957.

Some simple, some very complex poems illustrating the relationship of poetry, music, and the dance. Songs, singers, dance, instruments, composers, the power of music. Compiler's comments enhance one's understanding and enjoyment.

REED, GWENDOLYN, comp. *Out of the Ark,* An Anthology of Animal Verse. Drawings by GABRIELE MARGULES. New York: Atheneum Publishers, 1968.

A dignified collection of animal poems, few of which are found in children's anthologies. Many of the poems are quite old. The arrangement seems to group poems that are similar in effect.

WEISS, RENÉE KAROL. *A Paper Zoo,* A Collection of Animal Poems by Modern American Poets. Illustrations by ELLEN RASKIN. New York: Macmillan Co., 1968.

This choice of poems was originally made for so-called "culturally deprived" kindergarteners. The compiler felt that they deserved and "would respond to the very best in art."

C. Anthologies — Form, Country of Origin

BARON, VIRGINIA, ed. *The Seasons of Time,* Tanka Poetry of Ancient Japan. Illustrated by YASUHIDE KOBASHI. New York: Dial Press, 1968.

Tanka poetry is introduced with brush-and-ink illustrations that are Oriental in flavor. Somewhat similar to haiku, tanka often seems to be more personal.

BEHN, HARRY, comp. *Cricket Songs,* Japanese Haiku. With pictures selected from SESSHU and other Japanese masters. New York: Harcourt, Brace & World, 1964.

Lovely, browsable selection of haiku poetry. The translations retain the strict five-seven-five syllable form.

BREWTON, SARA and JOHN E. *Laughable Limericks.* Illustrated by INGRID FETZ. New York: Thomas Y. Crowell Co., 1965.

The humor ranges from slapstick to sophisticated, and there is an amazing variety of subjects about which limericks have been written.

CAUSLEY, CHARLES. *Modern Ballads and Story Poems.* Chosen and introduced by CHARLES CAUSLEY, with drawings by ANNE NETH-ERWOOD. New York: Franklin Watts, 1964.

The stories are more likely to be stark than humorous or adventurous. While more appropriate in secondary schools, some of the poems could be used with younger children. The collection has great force.

LEWIS, RICHARD, ed. *The Moment of Wonder,* A Collection of Chinese and Japanese poetry. Illustrated with paintings by Chinese and Japanese masters. New York: The Dial Press, 1964.

The editor's comments highlight this collection of Oriental poetry. There is variation in the length and form of the poems, which are grouped into categories concerning nature, landscapes, seasons, and man. As in the Behn volume, the authentic Oriental illustrations are reproduced only in black and white.

————. *In a Spring Garden.* Pictures by Ezra Jack Keats. New York: Dial Press, 1965.

Ezra Jack Keats' lovely full- and double-page spreads augment the haiku poetry. This is a true picture book, with illustrations as significant as the text.

Malcolmson, Anne. *Song of Robin Hood.* Boston: Houghton Mifflin Co., 1947.

A selection of some of the Robin Hood ballads, with each stanza illustrated in exquisite detail. Melodies are included. Excellent example of the blending of art, music, and literature.

Manning-Sanders, Ruth, comp. *A Bundle of Ballads.* Illustrated by William Stobbs. Philadelphia: J. B. Lippincott Co., 1959.

Many traditional ballads, only a few of which are found in anthologies. An excellent complement to *Modern Ballads and Story Poems.*

Parker, Elinor, ed. *100 Story Poems.* Illustrated by Henry C. Pitz. New York: Thomas Y. Crowell Co., 1951.

Very few traditional ballads — for the most part, those often anthologized. Book's primary usefulness would be as a basic collection of story poems. Few will browse through this but will more likely go to it for a well-defined purpose.

————. *100 More Story Poems.* Illustrated by Peter Spier. New York: Thomas Y. Crowell Co., 1960.

————. *The Singing and the Gold,* Poems Translated from World Literature. Wood engravings by Clare Leighton. New York: Thomas Y. Crowell Co., 1962.

The likeness of mankind becomes clear, and one discovers many new poets. Thirty-four languages are represented, but the arrangement is by subject rather than by country.

D. Anthologies — Traditional Lore, Children's Writing

Belting, Natalia. *Calendar Moon.* Illustrated by Bernarda Bryson. New York: Holt, Rinehart & Winston, 1964.

A collection of the expressions of various cultures concerning the months. Two or three poems of fair length for each month.

————. *The Sun Is a Golden Earring.* Illustrated by Bernarda Bryson. New York: Holt, Rinehart & Winston, 1962.

What men have said as they tried to understand the sky, the moon, the sun, storms, and the stars. The reader is invited to dream along with them "and match their thoughts to his own."

Doob, Leonard, ed. *A Crocodile Has Me by the Leg.* Illustrated by Solomon Irein Wangboje. New York: Walker & Co., 1966.

Illustrated by a Nigerian, this book of African folk rhymes contains verses which are not childlike but which reflect life as it is for the people.

LEWIS, RICHARD, ed. *Out of the Earth I Sing,* Poetry and Songs of Primitive People of the World. New York: W. W. Norton & Co., 1968.

A collection distinguished in every way. The selections, grouped according to similarity, are rich and lovely. Illustrations are photographs of primitive art. The editor notes the alertness to the natural world shown by these poems of primitive people, and also the fact that their literary roots are the roots of all literature.

——. *Miracles,* Poems by Children of the English-Speaking World. New York: Simon and Schuster, 1966.

A volume of poetry written by children of the entire English-speaking world. Handsome format.

——. *The Wind and the Rain,* Children's Poems. Photographs by HELEN BUTTFIELD. New York: Simon and Schuster, 1968.

A few short poems by children on weather elements. Photographs share honors with poems.

MARY-ROUSSELIERE, GUY. *Beyond the High Hills,* A Book of Eskimo Poems. Photos by GUY MARY-ROUSSELIERE. Cleveland: World Publishing Co., 1961.

The color photographs are poetry themselves. Traditional Eskimo poems are concerned with hunting, human relationships, eagerness to live.

MORRISON, LILLIAN, comp. *Touch Blue.* Signs and Spells; Love Charms and Chants; Auguries and Old Beliefs in Rhyme. Illustrated by Doris Lee. New York: Thomas Y. Crowell Co., 1958.

——. *Yours Till Niagara Falls.* Illustrated by MARJORIE BAUERN-SCHMIDT. New York: Thomas Y. Crowell Co., 1950.

——. *Remember Me when This You See,* A New Collection of Autograph Verses. Illustrated by MARJORIE BAUERNSCHMIDT. New York: Thomas Y. Crowell Co., 1961.

POTTER, CHARLES FRANCIS, comp. *Tongue Tanglers.* Illustrated by WILLIAM WIESNER. Cleveland: World Publishing Co., 1962.

This is useful in showing that words and their sounds are fun.

REES, ENNIS. *The Song of Paul Bunyan & Tony Beaver.* Illustrated by ROBERT OSBORN. New York: Pantheon Books, 1964.

Stories of each of these men and also of their confrontation with each other, told in natural speech rhythms.

STOUTENBERG, ADRIAN. *The Crocodile's Mouth,* Folk-Song Stories. Illustrated by GLEN ROUNDS. New York: Viking Press, 1966.

No music is included, but these have enough storyline to carry the songs. All are American by origin or adoption.

WITHERS, CARL, comp. *A Rocket in My Pocket,* The Rhymes and Chants of Young Americans. Illustrated by SUSANNE SUBA. New York: Holt, Rinehart & Winston, 1948.

Riddles, games, jokes, sayings that children learn to play. A favorite with children.

WOOD, RAY, comp. *The American Mother Goose.* Illustrated by ED HARGIS. Philadelphia: J. B. Lippincott Co., 1940.

Pictures of raggedy, homespun people accompany this gathering of traditional American rhymes of childhood.

WORSTELL, EMMA VIETOR. *Jump the Rope Jingles.* Illustrated by SHEILA GREENWALD. New York: Macmillan Co., 1961.

Traditional jump-rope rhymes, with directions for playing them.

E. Mother Goose Books

ANGLUND, JOAN. *In a Pumpkin Shell,* A Mother Goose ABC. New York: Harcourt, Brace & World, 1960.

BRIGGS, RAYMOND. *Mother Goose Treasury.* New York: Coward-McCann, 1966.

———. *Fee Fi Fo Fum,* A Picture Book of Nursery Rhymes. New York: Coward-McCann, 1964.

———. *Ring-a-Ring o' Roses.* New York: Coward-McCann, 1962.

———. *The White Land,* A Picture Book of Traditional Rhymes and Verses. New York: Coward-McCann, 1963.

BROOKE, L. LESLIE. *Little Bo-Peep. Man in the Moon. Oranges and Lemons. Ring o' Roses.* London: Frederick Warne & Co., n.d.

CALDECOTT, RANDOLPH R. *Caldecott's First Collection of Pictures and Songs. R. Caldecott's Second Collection of Pictures and Songs.* London: Frederick Warne & Co., n.d.

COONEY, BARBARA. *Mother Goose in French.* Translated by HUGH LATHAM. New York: Thomas Y. Crowell Co., 1964.

———. *Mother Goose in Spanish.* Translated by ALASTAIR REID and ANTHONY KERRIGAN. New York: Thomas Y. Crowell Co., 1968.

———. *Courtship, Merry Marriage, and Feast of Cock Robin and Jenny Wren,* to which is added The Doleful Death of Cock Robin. Illustrated by BARBARA COONEY. New York: Charles Scribner's Sons, 1965.

CRANE, WALTER. *The Baby's Opera,* A Book of Old Rhymes with New Dresses. London: Frederick Warne & Co., n.d.

DE ANGELI, MARGUERITE. *Book of Nursery and Mother Goose Rhymes.* Garden City, N.Y.: Doubleday & Co., 1954.

EMBERLEY, BARBARA, adaptor. *Drummer Hoff.* Illustrated by ED EMBERLEY. Englewood Cliffs, N.J.: Prentice-Hall, 1967.

FRASCONI, ANTONIO. *The House that Jack Built,* A Picture Book in Two Languages. New York: Harcourt, Brace & World, 1958.

GALDONE, PAUL. *Old Mother Hubbard and Her Dog.* Pictures by PAUL GALDONE. New York: McGraw-Hill Book Co., 1960.

GREENAWAY, KATE. *Mother Goose,* or The Old Nursery Rhymes. London: Frederick Warne & Co., 1881.

HALEY, GAIL E. *One Two, Buckle My Shoe,* A Book of Counting Rhymes. Illustrated by GAIL E. HALEY. Garden City, N.Y.: Doubleday & Co., 1964.

KAPP, PAUL. *A Cat Came Fiddling* and Other Rhymes of Childhood. Adapted and made into songs by PAUL KAPP. Illustrated by IRENE HAAS. New York: Harcourt, Brace & World, 1956.

LINES, KATHLEEN, comp. *Lavender's Blue,* A Book of Nursery Rhymes. Pictures by HAROLD JONES. New York: Franklin Watts, 1954.

MONTGOMERIE, NORAH, comp. *This Little Pig Went to Market; Play Rhymes.* Illustrated by MARGERY GILL. New York: Franklin Watts, 1967.

OPIE, IONA and PETER, comp. *The Oxford Nursery Rhyme Book.* Assembled by Iona and Peter Opie. Additional illustrations by JOAN HASSALL. Oxford: The Clarendon Press, 1963.

REED, PHILIP. *Mother Goose and Nursery Rhymes.* New York: Atheneum Publishers, 1963.

SMITH, JESSIE WILLCOX. *The Little Mother Goose.* With numerous illustrations in full color and black and white. New York: Dodd, Mead & Co., 1918.

SPIER, PETER. *London Bridge Is Falling Down!.* Illustrated by PETER SPIER. Garden City, N.Y.: Doubleday & Co., 1967.

TUDOR, TASHA. *Mother Goose.* Seventy-seven verses, with pictures by TASHA TUDOR. New York: Henry Z. Walck, 1944.

WILDSMITH, BRIAN. *Brian Wildsmith's Mother Goose,* A Collection of Nursery Rhymes. New York: Franklin Watts, 1964.

WINSOR, FREDERICK. *The Space Child's Mother Goose.* Illustrated by MARIAN PARRY. New York: Simon and Schuster, 1958.

WRIGHT, BLANCHE. *The Real Mother Goose.* Chicago: Rand McNally & Co., 1916.

F. Source Books for Nursery Rhymes

BARING-GOULD, WILLIAM S. and CEIL. *The Annotated Mother Goose,* Nursery Rhymes Old and New, Arranged and Explained. Illustrated by WALTER CRANE, RANDOLPH CALDECOTT, KATE GREENAWAY, ARTHUR RACKHAM, MAXFIELD PARRISH, and early historical woodcuts. With chapter decorations by E. M. Simon. New York: Clarkson N. Potter, 1962.

OPIE, IONA and PETER. *Oxford Dictionary of Nursery Rhymes.* Oxford: The Clarendon Press, 1951.

G. Books by One Poet

AIKEN, CONRAD. *Cats and Bats and Things with Wings.* Drawings by MILTON GLASER. New York: Atheneum Publishers, 1965.

ALDIS, DOROTHY. *All Together,* A Child's Treasury of Verse. Illustrations by HELEN D. JAMESON, MARJORIE FLACK, and MARGARET FREEMAN. New York: G. P. Putnam's Sons, 1952.

BARNSTONE, ALIKI. *The Real Tin Flower*, Poems About the World at Nine. Drawings by PAUL GIOVANAPOULAS. New York: Simon and Schuster, 1966.

BEHN, HARRY. *The Golden Hive*. Poems and pictures by HARRY BEHN. New York: Harcourt, Brace & World, 1966.

———. *The Little Hill*. Poems and pictures by HARRY BEHN. New York: Harcourt, Brace & World, 1949.

———. *The Wizard in the Well*. Poems and pictures by HARRY BEHN. New York: Harcourt Brace Jovanovich, Inc., 1956.

BELLOC, HILAIRE. *The Bad Child's Book of Beasts*. Pictures by B.T.B. New York: Alfred A. Knopf, 1965.

———. *Cautionary Verses*. Pictures by B.T.B. and NICOLAS BENTLEY. New York: Alfred A. Knopf, 1968.

BENET, ROSEMARY and STEPHEN VINCENT. *A Book of Americans*. Illustrations by CHARLES CHILD. New York: Holt, Rinehart & Winston, 1961.

BLAKE, WILLIAM. *Songs of Innocence*. Music and illustrations by Ellen Raskin. Garden City, N.Y.: Doubleday & Co., 1966.

BROWN, MARGARET W. *Nibble Nibble*, Poems for Children. Illustrations by Leonard Weisgard. New York: William R. Scott, 1959.

CIARDI, JOHN. *I Met a Man*. Illustrated by ROBERT OSBORN. Boston: Houghton Mifflin Co., 1961.

———. *The Man Who Sang the Sillies*. Drawings by EDWARD GOREY. Philadelphia: J. B. Lippincott, 1961.

———. *The Reason for the Pelican*. Illustrated by MADELEINE GEKIERE. Philadelphia: J. B. Lippincott, 1959.

———. *The Monster Den*, or Look What Happened at My House—and To It. Drawings by EDWARD GOREY. Philadelphia: J. B. Lippincott, 1966.

———. *You Know Who*. Drawings by EDWARD GOREY. Philadelphia: J. B. Lippincott, 1964.

———. *You Read to Me, I'll Read to You*. Drawings by EDWARD GOREY. New York: J. B. Lippincott, 1962.

CLARK, ANN. *Little Herder in Spring*. Illustrated by HOKE DENETSOSIE. Washington, D. C.: U. S. Dept. of the Interior, Bureau of Indian Affairs, n.d.

———. *Little Herder in Summer*. Illustrated by HOKE DENETSOSIE. Washington, D. C.: U. S. Dept. of the Interior, Bureau of Indian Affairs, n.d.

COATSWORTH, ELIZABETH. *Poems*. Decorations by VEE GUTHRIE. New York: Macmillan Co., 1958.

DE LA MARE, WALTER. *Rhymes and Verses*, Collected Poems for Children. With drawings by ELINORE BLAISDELL. New York: Holt, Rinehart & Winston, 1947.

————. *Bells and Grass*. Illustrations by DOROTHY LATHROP. New York: Viking Press, 1961.

————. *Peacock Pie*. Illustrations by BARBARA COONEY. New York: Alfred A. Knopf, 1961.

ELIOT, T. S. *Old Possum's Book of Practical Cats*. Decorations by NICOLAS BENTLEY. New York: Harcourt, Brace & World, 1967.

FISHER, AILEEN. *Cricket in a Thicket*. Illustrated by FEODOR ROJANKOVSKY. New York: Charles Scribner's Sons, 1963.

FLANDERS, MICHAEL. *Creatures Great and Small*. Illustrated by MARCELLO MINALE. New York: Holt, Rinehart & Winston, 1964.

FROST, ROBERT. *You Come Too*, Favorite Poems for Young Readers. Wood engravings by THOMAS W. NASON. New York: Holt, Rinehart & Winston, 1959.

HUBBELL, PATRICIA. *The Apple Vendor's Fair*. Drawings by JULIE MAAS. New York: Atheneum Publishers, 1963.

————. *Catch Me a Wind*. Drawings by SUSAN TROMMLER. New York: Atheneum Publishers, 1968.

JOHNSON, DORIS. *A Cloud of Summer*, and Other New Haiku. Illustrated by W. T. MARS. Chicago: Follett Publishing Co., 1967.

JOHNSON, SIDDIE JOE. *Feather in My Hand*. Drawings by BARBARA J. McGEE. New York: Atheneum Publishers, 1967.

LEAR, EDWARD. *The Complete Nonsense Book*. New York: Dodd, Mead & Co., 1964.

LEWIS, CLAUDIA. *Poems of Earth and Space*. Illustrations by SYMEON SHIMIN. New York: E. P. Dutton & Co., 1967.

LEWIS, RICHARD. *Of This World*, A Poet's Life in Poetry. Photographs by HELEN BUTTFIELD. New York: Dial Press, 1968.

LIVINGSTON, MYRA COHN. *The Moon and a Star and Other Poems*. Illustrations by JUDITH SHAHN. New York: Harcourt Brace Jovanovich, Inc., 1965.

————. *I'm Hiding*. Illustrations by ERIK BLEGVAD. New York: Harcourt, Brace & World, 1961.

————. *Whispers and Other Poems*. Illustrations by JACQUELINE CHAST. New York: Harcourt, Brace & World, 1958.

McCORD, DAVID. *Every Time I Climb a Tree*. Illustrated by MARC SIMONT. Boston: Little, Brown & Co., 1967.

————. *Far and Few*, Rhymes of the Never Was and Always Is. Drawings by HENRY B. KANE. Boston: Little, Brown & Co., 1952.

————. *All Day Long*, Fifty Rhymes of the Never Was and Always Is. Drawings by HENRY B. KANE. Boston: Little, Brown & Co., 1966.

————. *Take Sky*, More Rhymes of the Never Was and Always Is. Drawings by HENRY B. KANE. Boston: Little, Brown & Co., 1962.

MERRIAM, EVE. *Catch a Little Rhyme*. Pictures by IMERO GOBBATO. New York: Atheneum Publishers, 1966.

———. *It Doesn't Always Have to Rhyme.* Drawings by MALCOLM
SPOONER. New York: Atheneum Publishers, 1964.

———. *There Is No Rhyme for Silver.* Drawings by JOSEPH SCHINDEL-
MAN. New York: Atheneum Publishers, 1962.

MILNE, A. A. *When We Were Very Young.* New York: E. P. Dutton
& Co., 1924.

———. *Now We Are Six.* With decorations by ERNEST H. SHEPARD.
New York: E. P. Dutton & Co., 1927.

———. *The World of Christopher Robin; The Complete When We
Were Very Young and Now We Are Six.* Decorations and new full
color illustrations by ERNEST H. SHEPARD. New York: E. P.
Dutton & Co., 1958.

———. *The Christopher Robin Book of Verse.* Decorations and illustrations in color by ERNEST H. SHEPARD. New York: E. P. Dutton & Co., 1967.

———. *The Pooh Song Book.* Words by A. A. Milne. Music by H.
FRAZER-SIMSON. Decorations by ERNEST H. SHEPARD. New York:
E. P. Dutton & Co., 1961.

MIZUMURA, KAZUE. *I See the Winds.* New York: Thomas Y. Crowell
Co., 1966.

MOORE, JOHN TRAVERS. *Cinnamon Seed.* Illustrations by TRINA
SCHART HYMAN. Boston: Houghton Mifflin Co., 1967.

MOORE, LILIAN. *I Feel the Same Way.* Illustrations by ROBERT
QUACKENBUSH. New York: Atheneum Publishers, 1967.

NEVILLE, MARY. *Woody and Me.* Pictures by RONNI SOLBERT. New
York: Pantheon Books, 1966.

O'NEILL, MARY. *Hailstones and Halibut Bones,* Adventures in Color.
Illustrated by LEONARD WEISGARD. Garden City, N.Y.: Doubleday & Co., 1961.

———. *Words, Words, Words.* Decorations by JUDY PIUSSI-CAMPBELL.
Garden City, N.Y.: Doubleday & Co., 1966.

———. *What Is That Sound?* Drawings by LOIS EHLERT. New York:
Atheneum Publishers, 1966.

PRELUTSKY, JACK. *A Gopher in the Garden* and Other Animal Poems.
Pictures by ROBERT LEYDENFROST. New York: Macmillan Co.,
1967.

REEVES, JAMES. *The Blackbird in the Lilac,* Verses for Children. Illustrated by EDWARD ARDIZZONE. New York: E. P. Dutton & Co.,
1959.

RIEU, E. V. *The Flattered Flying Fish and Other Poems.* Illustrations
by ERNEST H. SHEPARD. New York: E. P. Dutton & Co., 1962.

ROSSETTI, CHRISTINA. *Sing-Song, A Nursery Rhyme Book for Children.*
Illustrations by MARGUERITE DAVIS. New York: Macmillan Co.,
1924.

SANDBURG, CARL. *Early Moon*. Illustrations by JAMES DAUGHERTY. New York: Harcourt, Brace & World, 1958.

——. *Wind Song*. Illustrations by WILLIAM A. SMITH. New York: Harcourt, Brace & World, 1960.

SHAKESPEARE, WILLIAM. *Seeds of Time* (Selections from SHAKE-SPEARE). Compiled by BERNICE GROHSKOPF. Drawings by KELLY OECHSLI. New York: Atheneum Publishers, 1693.

SMITH, WILLIAM JAY. *Laughing Time*. Illustrations by JULIET KEPES. Boston: Little, Brown & Co., 1955.

——. *Typewriter Town*. New York: E. P. Dutton & Co., 1960.

——. *Mr. Smith & Other Nonsense*. Pictures by DON BOLOGNESE. New York: Delacorte Press, 1968.

STARBIRD, KAY. *The Pheasant on Route Seven*. Illustrations by VIC-TORIA DE LARREA. Philadelphia: J. B. Lippincott Co., 1968.

——. *Don't Ever Cross a Crocodile, and Other Poems*. Illustrations by KIT DALTON. Philadelphia: J. B. Lippincott Co., 1963.

——. *A Snail's a Failure Socially, and Other Poems Mostly About People*. Illustrations by KIT DALTON. Philadalphia: J. B. Lippincott Co., 1966.

STEVENSON, ROBERT LOUIS. *A Child's Garden of Verses*. Many editions from which to choose.

SWENSON, MAY. *Poems to Solve*. New York: Charles Scribner's Sons, 1966.

TAGORE, RABINDRANATH. *Moon, For What Do You Wait?* Illustrated by ASHLEY BRYAN. New York: Atheneum Publishers, 1967.

TEASDALE, SARA. *Stars Tonight,* Verses New and Old for Boys and Girls. Illustrated by DOROTHY P. LATHROP. New York: Macmillan Co., 1930.

H. Books with a Single Poem

BISHOP, ELIZABETH. *Ballad of the Burglar of Babylon*. Woodcuts by ANN GRIFALCONI. New York: Farrar, Straus & Giroux, 1968.

FISHER, AILEEN. *Going Barefoot*. Illustrated by ADRIENNE ADAMS. New York: Thomas Y. Crowell Co., 1960.

——. *In the Middle of the Night*. Illustrated by ADRIENNE ADAMS. New York: Thomas Y. Crowell Co., 1965.

——. *Where Does Everyone Go?* Illustrated by ADRIENNE ADAMS. New York: Thomas Y. Crowell Co., 1961.

LONGFELLOW, HENRY WADSWORTH. *Paul Revere's Ride*. Illustrated by PAUL GALDONE. New York: Thomas Y. Crowell Co., 1963. (See also HOPKINSON, FRANCIS. *The Battle of the Kegs*. Illus-trated by PAUL GALDONE. New York: Thomas Y. Crowell Co., 1964.)

LUND, DORIS HEROLD. *Attic of the Wind*. Illustrated by CETI FOR-
BERG. New York: Parents' Magazine Press, 1966.

STEEGMULLER, FRANCIS, and GUTERMAN, NORBERT. *Papillot, Clignot
et Dodo*. Freely translated into French from the English of
EUGENE FIELD's *Wynken, Blynken and Nod*. Illustrated by BAR-
BARA COONEY. New York: Farrar, Straus & Giroux, 1964.

TENNYSON, ALFRED LORD. *The Charge of the Light Brigade*. Illustrated by ALICE and MARTIN PROVENSEN. New York: Golden
Press, 1964.

THAYER, ERNEST LAWRENCE. *Casey at the Bat*. Illustrated by PAUL
FRAME. Englewood Cliffs, N. J.: Prentice-Hall, 1965.

II. Audiovisual Materials

    A. Sources that Evaluate Audiovisual Materials

       American Record Guide. Published by the American Record Guide,
       Inc., P.O. Box 319, Radio City Station, New York 10019. Month-
       ly.

       Annotated List of Recordings in the Language Arts. National Council
       of Teachers of English, 508 S. Sixth St., Champaign, Illinois
       68120. $1.75, 1964.

       Audio Cardalog. Box 989, Larchmont, New York 10538. Monthly
       (Sept.-June) Index every six months.

       Audiovisual Instruction. Published by Department of Audiovisual In-
       struction, NEA, 1201 16th St., N.W., Washington, D. C. 20036.
       Ten issues per year.

       EFLA Evaluations. Educational Film Library Association, Inc., 250
       W. 57th St., New York 10019. Available only to members.

       Educational Screen and Audiovisual Guide. Published by Educational
       Screen, Inc., 434 S. Wabash Ave., Chicago, Illinois 60605.
       Monthly.

       Film Library Quarterly. Published by Film Library Information Coun-
       cil, 101 W. Putnam Ave., Greenwich, Conn. 06830. Quarterly
       — March, June, September, December.

       The Instructor. Published by Instructor Publications, Inc., Instructor
       Park, Dansville, New York 14437. Ten issues a year.

       Landers Film Reviews. Published by Landers Associates, P. O. Box
       69760, Los Angeles, Calif. 90069. Monthly (except July and
       August).

       Recordings for Children: A Selected List. New York Library Associa-
       tion, Children's and Young Adult Services Section, P. O. Box
       521, Woodside, New York 11377. $1.00, 1964, rev. ed.

    B. Non-Evaluative Sources

       Blue Book of Audiovisual Material. Educational Screen and Audio-
       visual Guide, 434 S. Wabash Ave., Chicago, Illinois 60605.
       August of each year.

National Information Center for Educational Media. *Index to 8mm Motion Cartridges*. New York: R. R. Bowker Company, 1969.

———. *Index to Overhead Transparencies*. New York: R.̄ R. Bowker Company, 1969.

———. *Index to 16mm Educational Films*, 2d ed. New York: R. R. Bowker Company, 1969.

———. *Index to 35mm Educational Filmstrips*, 2d ed., New York: R. R. Bowker Company, 1969.

SLJ Audiovisual Guide: A Multimedia Subject List. School Library Journal, R. R. Bowker Co., 1180 Avenue of the Americas, New York. 10036.

Forthcoming releases (selected media) with complete bibliographic information and annotations. Semi-annual. (Appears in April and November issues.)

C. Recommended Audiovisual Textbooks

BROWN, JAMES W.; LEWIS, RICHARD B.; and HARCLEROAD, FRED F. *AV Instruction: Media and Methods*, 3d ed. New York: McGraw-Hill Book Co., 1969.

DALE, EDGAR. *Audiovisual Methods in Teaching*. 3d ed. New York: Holt, Rinehart & Winston, 1969.

ERICKSON, CARLTON W. H. *Fundamentals of Teaching with Audiovisual Technology*. New York: Macmillan Co., 1965.

WITTICH, WALTER ARNO, and SCHULLER, CHARLES FRANCIS. *Audiovisual Materials: Their Nature and Use*. New York: Harper & Row, Publishers, 1967.

D. Selective List of Poems in Audiovisual Format

1. Records

An Anthology of Negro Poetry for Young People. Compiled and read by ARNA BONTEMPS. Folkways Records FC 7114, 1958.

Anthology of Negro Poets. Edited by ARNA BONTEMPS. Readings by LANGSTON HUGHES, STERLING BROWN, CLAUD McKAY, COUNTEE CULLEN, GWENDOLYN BROOKS, and MARGARET WALKER. Folkways Records FL 9791, 1966.

Anthology of Negro Poets in the U.S.A. – 200 Years. Read by ARNA BONTEMPS. Folkways Records FL 9792, 1955.

An Anthology of Poetry for Children. Read by CECIL BELLAMY, HARVEY HALL, JOAN HART, DAVID KING, PENELOPE LEE, ANN MORRISH, and PETER ORR. Directed by PETER ORR. Spoken Arts 977, 1967.

Carl Sandburg's Poems for Children. Read by CARL SANDBURG. Caedmon TC 1124, n.d.

A Child's Garden of Verses. Read by JUDITH ANDERSON. Caedmon TC 1077, 1957.

Miracles. Poems Written by Children. Collected by RICHARD LEWIS. Read by JULIE HARRIS and RODDY McDOWALL. Caedmon TC 1227, 1967.

Mother Goose. Features CYRIL RITCHARD, CELESTE HOLM, and BORIS KARLOFF. Directed by HOWARD O. SACKLER, with music by HERSHY KAY. Caedmon TC 1091, 1958.

The Pied Piper and The Hunting of the Snark. Read by BORIS KARLOFF. Caedmon TC 1075, 1960.

Poetry Parade, Poets Read Their Poetry for Children. Edited by NANCY LARRICK. DAVID McCORD and HARRY BEHN, WW 703. KARLA KUSKIN and AILEEN FISHER. WW 704. Weston Woods Studios, 1967. (2-record album).

Poetry Programs for Children, Vol. I. A dramatic presentation created and performed by ELEANOR BASESCU. CMS Records, Inc., 506, 1966.

Poetry Programs for Children, Vol. III. For upper elementary grades 4-7. Performed by ELEANOR BASESCU. CMS Records, Inc., 350, 1966.

Reflections on a Gift of Watermelon Pickle . . . and Other Modern Verse. STEPHEN DUNNING, EDWARD LUEDERS, and HUGH SMITH, comps. Read by ELLEN HOLLY and PAUL HECHT. Scholastic Records FS 11007, 1967.

T. S. Eliot Reads Old Possum's Book of Practical Cats. Argo RG 116, n.d.

Treasury of Lewis Carroll. Read and sung by CHRISTOPHER CASSON. Spoken Arts SA 897, n.d.

Treasury of Nursery Rhymes. Sung and read by CHRISTOPHER CASSON. Presented by ARTHUR LUCE KLEIN. Vol. 1 and 2. Spoken Arts SA 857 and 885, 1963.

UNTERMEYER, LOUIS. *Discovering Rhythm and Rhyme in Poetry.* Read by JULIE HARRIS and DAVID WAYNE. Caedmon TC 1156, 1967.

2. Filmstrips

In a Spring Garden. — Attic of the Wind. — Casey at the Bat. — The Owl and the Pussy cat. — Wynken, Blynken and Nod. — Custard the Dragon. Weston Woods Studios sound filmstrip, Set 13, n.d. (Record or filmstrips may be purchased separately.)

3. Films

The Day Is Two Feet Long. Weston Woods Studios, 9 min., color, 1968.

Hailstones and Halibut Bones. Sterling Educational Films, (241 East 34th St., New York 10016). Part I., 1964, 6 min., color. Part II., 1967, 7 min., color.

In a Spring Garden. Pictures by EZRA JACK KEATS. Narrated by RICHARD LEWIS. Weston Woods Studios, 6 min., color, n.d.

London Bridge Is Falling Down. Connecticut Films, Inc., (6 Cobble Hill Road, Westport 06880), sound, color, 10 min. (approx.), 1969.

Poetry to Grow On. Grover Film Production, (P. O. Box 303, Monterey, Calif.), 16mm sound, color, 18 1/2 min. 1966.

Poems We Write. Grover Film Production, 1968. 16mm sound, color, 15 min.

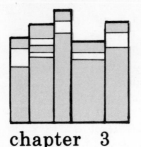

chapter 3

poets and pedagogues

The Poetry Program

The poetry program is based on a belief in poetry, that it can enhance lives, and that it is not particularly esoteric. It is likewise based on a belief in children, young people who bring so much to poetry and who can take so much from it. It requires a perceptive and knowledgeable leader who realizes that his first job is to keep poetry enjoyable for children.

Two problems need to be faced at the outset. The first is that what has been done with poetry in the past has tended to drive people from it. Poetry has borne the brunt of what actually is the fault of the presenters of poetry. An awareness of pitfalls to be avoided is necessary to the adult who would successfully bring poetry to children. As a starter, it may be well to look back on one's own experiences with poetry. It is to be hoped that there were some good ones, but one can be almost certain that there were some that were quite negative.

The second problem results from the first. Many people who were turned away from poetry as children are very unenthusiastic as adults and see no particular reason to bother with poetry. Therefore, they completely avoid it. This in itself is perhaps less dangerous than misusing poetry, but it has the same effect of depriving children of the pleasures of poetry.

The poetry program can and should take place in an environment where the development of the child as a feeling and thinking being is the paramount end. If the individual is more important than the curriculum, if stimulation is prized above the learning of facts, if communication is more vital than busy work, then poetry not only can exist, but it can actively be sought after by the teacher as an intrinsic part of the total educational process.

The term *poetry program* implies planning, a structure, and regularity. It means having objectives, knowing possible approaches which can be evaluated and adapted, and having the ability to develop one's own program. It means knowing poetry and knowing children. (Unfortunately, it may imply something cut and dried that can be planned fully the first year in late August and then used unchanged each year until retirement.) If poetry is to be more than a mental picture of what a poem looks like, we must combine the best of the educator and the humanist.

Too often, teachers of poetry fall into two categories. At one extreme is the person who believes that it is enough merely to expose children to good poetry. At the other extreme is the one who "teaches poems."

The teacher in the first category feels that by doing any more than merely exposing children to poetry makes it a chore and something too impersonal to mean anything, that it actually ruins poetry for children. While this attitude is not without some validity, it leaves too much to chance. It is naive and wishful thinking to assume that all children could intuitively fully appreciate poetry.

A student of children's literature once remarked, "But if the poet has done his job well, the child will realize what the poet is striving for." However, few people are as perceptive as they could be, even children. Nor do we all listen or read carefully. A teacher can (and ought to) do things with (not to) children that will heighten awareness and make future poetry more accessible and meaningful. The helpful comment, the thought-provoking question, the permissive discussion, the choice of poems, and the stimulating activity all can enhance poetry. A good teacher opens doors to poetry.

Those who would do no more than make poetry available to children are probably reacting to the other extreme—the adult who "teaches poems." Each poem is discussed, analyzed, interpreted for children. It's all business, no enjoyment. This is downright harmful. Few normal youngsters would ever voluntarily seek out poetry after such treatment.

The problem then becomes this: To what extent will we introduce poetry with minimal comment, and what will we do in the way of formalized activities? There will never be a single correct answer to this. The only solution is the one each individual teacher finds that works for his group.

The reader would be wise to gather the ideas of many people on using poetry with children to see what some of the differing positions and possibilities are. (See Selected References, Part I.)

The classroom and the school should be richly stocked with poetry which is made easily available. Poetry is part of everyday life, neither to be set on a pedestal nor to be ignored. It is recommended that the teacher read poems daily and have frequent poetry sessions, and that children listen to, read, view, and write poetry.

Objectives

With poetry, one must start with the children where they are, or at any rate, where they can comfortably keep up. A teacher must ask himself: What are my objectives for this year for this group? Then he should write them down, revise them when necessary, and continue to rethink what he is working toward. (This will be based on his rationale for using poetry, which also needs to be spelled out.)

As a guide to formulating objectives, the following summary may be helpful. In the area of perception, one can provide and encourage experiences with the hope of being successful in developing these understandings.

PERCEPTS

1. Poetry is enjoyable and is to be desired. However, not all poems are equally enjoyed, and some will actively be disliked.
2. A poem speaks to the individual, who reads and interprets it in terms of his life.
3. Poetry can have impact on the life of the listener through what it suggests to him and brings out in him.

While emphasizing a feeling for poetry, more specific concepts about poetry should be developed.

CONCEPTS

1. Poetry is poetry because of its distinguishing qualities:
   a. language, melody
   b. experience
   c. emotion
   d. compression
   e. rhythm
   f. communication
2. Poems have been written by many people; they can take many forms; and they can be about almost any subject imaginable.
3. Poetry is available in many places and forms, and the user knows how to find the poetry he wants.

There is no point to all this without action on the part of the child.

BEHAVIOR

1. Poetry is voluntarily read/heard.
2. The knowledge of poetry as a literary genre, and past experience with poetry, lead to deepening appreciation of poems encountered.

3. Poetry can effectively be shared orally.
4. The child writes poetry for his own personal satisfaction.

What will the teacher do to achieve his objectives? What activities will he use? What poems does he want to be sure to include? What materials does he want to make or order?

Along with planning ahead, the humanist in the teacher must always be able to change, to recognize and to take advantage of opportunities as they arise to bring in poetry. Flexibility and openness are as essential as planning.

The specific suggestions offered below are starting points for the beginner and are meant to serve as aids to the person who is hesitant about developing a poetry program. These ideas are to be reacted to and incorporated, adapted, or rejected accordingly. More important, the user will go beyond what he reads to develop his own approaches to the bringing together of children and poetry.

The danger of providing definite techniques is that these may be taken too seriously, be followed too blindly, and be considered as the last word. The introducer of poetry needs to be as creative as the poet.

Selection of Poems

In Chapter 2, the selection of poetry media was discussed. A further process is needed to choose the poems that will be shared with children. A good deal of the dislike for poetry has been based on poor selection of poems to be presented to children.

Appeal

The first criterion must be: Is this poem likely to appeal to my children? What makes it appeal? Children are drawn to what they can understand. Poetry that relates to their experiences and interests is essential. The eight-year-old is not particularly concerned with expressions of romantic love or with a mother's reaction to finding her grown son's teddy bear. Theodore Roosevelt, or Ireland in the spring, are not of the preschooler's world, and thus are likely to be tuned out.

And yet to limit poetry only to what children have experienced would be unfortunate. Poetry can help to extend experience. Never to go beyond the known is merely to mark time. It is advisable to include poetry that, while somehow pertaining to the child's world, also goes beyond it. In order that the child may extract any meaning from a poem, he must somehow relate the poem to his own personal frame of reference.

Must every poem be understood? Some never will be. Fine poetry leaves much for the partaker to unravel. What is mysterious to one child may be full of meaning to another. Furthermore, we must give children something to ponder.

Children should be given poetry from *their* world, poetry that is likely to speak to them; and they should be given some poetry that goes beyond their world, but that may also speak to them. However, to retain and expand interest in poetry, we must primarily use poetry that is meaningful to children now. (How many obscure poems could be tackled? A small number may be intriguing, but eventually may prove to be discouraging.)

Known interests of the child should be considered in making selections. Poems of animals, hobbies, humor, action, and suspense are likely to be well-received. It is not difficult to notice what children are doing and talking about, and then find appropriate poems.

It is a good idea to read research studies on children's poetry preferences. One may argue with the manner in which children are presented poems to which they are to react, but some studies do yield useful information as to which poems and poets children do enjoy.

A most ambitious study (over half the book is about poetry) knocks down many idols, and this fact may result in more discouragement than enlightenment. And yet one should not miss reading Norvell's *What Boys and Girls Like to Read*,[1] which brings out two primary findings: (1) children's choices are determined largely by content; (2) children's literature specialists, teachers, librarians, and anthologists don't really *know* what poems children like!

The understanding of maturity as a factor in determining choice of materials is another consideration. When is a group of children ready for a particular poem? Some poems are grown into, but others can be outgrown. The young child needs Mother Goose; an older child is likely to reject these rhymes. Many good poems, in effect, grow with the child.

Often, women teachers and women in training for teaching are drawn to that which is merely cute, that is, cute to an adult female. There are the poems that are sentimental, the ones that are "baby talk," ones *about* children rather than *for* them, and the poems that tell about "precious" children. If one keeps in mind those all-boy types of pupils, such unfortunate choices may be avoided.

A teacher makes preliminary judgments as to what poems to share on the basis of observation and general knowledge about children. Then he must try out his decisions on the critics to see where he has anticipated correctly and where he needs to revise. An alertness to children and an openness to their comments will yield the sought for reactions.

---

[1]George Norvell, *What Boys and Girls Like to Read* (Morristown, N. J.: Silver Burdett Company, 1958).

The glazed eye, the wriggling body, a smirk are some of the indications that one has chosen incorrectly, while smiles, intent looks, and noticeable quiet signal successful choices.

Variety is vital to introducing and maintaining interest in poetry. Humor may be a way into poetry for the uninterested child, but an excessive exposure to humorous rhymes and poems could result in a warped perspective of poetry. Poems of nature, activity, magic, beauty, feelings, families, the sea, nonsense, history, and so forth must be introduced to children. The individual child must be helped to find what poetry is, and to respond to a wide range of human experience through poetry. Not only subjects, but authors and forms of poetry need to be explored. The child can't be interested in something to which he has never been exposed.

Poems are chosen in relation to each other. What poems have children been introduced to? Which ones did they particularly enjoy? Which ones were neglected? In choosing a series of poems to use, it is well to be aware of the total combination. Do the poems that were chosen vary in depth, difficulty, approach? Poems differ in their audience. Among the poems selected, can any child find at least a few especially for him? Poems are chosen for a class, but they are also chosen for the individuals in the class.

The content of a poem—its subject and comprehensibility—helps to determine whether or not it will be used. It seems likely that if we can't hook children at the literal level, we'll miss out entirely. Poetry is far more than "What happens?", but our first reactions tend to be at this superficial level.

Literary Quality

The skill of the poet is similarly of great importance as a criterion in selecting poetry.[2] This is much more difficult to judge, and there aren't the clues of children's reactions to indicate whether or not one is heading in the right direction. Thoughtful experience (i.e. reading and reacting to poems) and reading what other people are saying about poetry seem to be all one can do on his own.

In evaluating the poem as literature, one might consider these questions:

Is it good poetry? Good verse?
Is it rhythmical but not over-rhythmical?

---

[2]Norvell found that literary quality was of negative importance in finding children's poetry interests. His reaction is to give them what they want. It seems wiser to find poems that combine quality and appeal. To present a poem that has only literary merit to recommend it is to continue to make a chore of poetry, and yet we owe children more than just appeal.

Does the author make rich use of language through his choice and arrangement of words, his use of metaphor and simile, alliteration, imagery, rhyme (if used)?

Does he bring life to what he writes about? Is the poem capable of evoking a response in the reader?

Does he suggest more than he says? (There are, however, some rhymes and jingles that may not do this; and yet it would be unfortunate if children were to miss out on these particular verses.) Is he sparing in his use of words?

Does the language flow smoothly and naturally, and does it translate to speech easily? Is the sound melodic?

Does increasing familiarity with a poem add to one's understanding and liking of it? (After years of reading aloud to children, the writer is convinced that the ultimate test of a work of literature is that it can be reread countless times, not only with original pleasure for the ever-changing audience, but with continuing pleasure for the reader.)

Is the style appropriate to the subject?

Judging the totality of a poem, what impact is it likely to have? Does it further our objectives for the poetry program? (Since the most important single objective is to develop an enjoyment of poetry, this is not so fearsome a criterion as it may sound.)

Educators freely state—and sometimes observe—the principle of starting with the child where he is. In poetry, this is essential. The young child is sure to be responsive to poetry. Mother Goose and simple poems are most appropriate for him.

While it is not a natural phenomenon, too many children become disenchanted with poetry or never encounter it as they go through school. With these older children, the first job is to try to change their attitude toward poetry. This will probably mean poetry with humor, an appealing storyline, suspense. (It will also mean an appealing presentation.)

As children's interest is captured, poems of greater depth and more variety can be added; there can be more concern with developing interests and not with just meeting those already established.

After all the sensible things are said, it must be pointed out that children will accept with delight an amazing number and variety of poems, more so than we suspect. In an afterword to *A Paper Zoo*, A Collection of Animal Poems by Modern American Poets, Renée Karol Weiss says that she used these poems with kindergarteners we would tend to call deprived children. They did respond to her choices (including T. S. Eliot, Marianne Moore, and Theodore Roethke), and very likely will respond in new ways as they mature. On the other hand, the fourth grader who has never heard "The House that Jack Built" may be more taken by it than the first grader. Stolid children may be moved by a poem of beauty such as Harry Behn's "Tree Song." Not all active boys will be unresponsive to the introspection reflected in Ann Nolan Clark's poems about the little herder.

We try to anticipate what will have appeal and meaning to children. But we must also have great respect for their innate capabilities and understanding.

The teacher's personal taste will dictate some of the choice of poems. His enthusiasm, his rapport with the class, and his manner of presentation may make a success of a poem that others could not put across.

Poetry Written Expressly for Children: Yes or No?

A perennial argument is whether or not to use the poetry of those who write expressly for children. Some feel that this will give youngsters an improper, inadequate concept of poetry that will have to be unlearned later on. They claim that children should have "adult" poetry from the beginning and not have their time wasted on poetry written just for them.

It is strange that this argument is rarely used for the reading of the novel. Apparently picture books and children's fiction are acceptable before reading adult novels, but we cannot allow for childhood in poetry. This seems specious. It appears that people who disapprove of children's poetry are usually those who have limited contact with real live children, and this fact may help explain their stand.

The poor quality, historically speaking, no doubt has had some bearing on such pronouncements against children's poetry. Children were not respected in the past; condescension and didacticism marked all writing for them. Even now, collections of rhymes appear that are simplistic rather than simple, condescending in a modern vein, limiting rather than exciting. Through careful selection, one can avoid these books and choose the ones that are well done; the proverbial baby need not be thrown out with the bathwater.

The fact is that children are not adults, and their uniquenesses ought to be provided for in poetry as it is in other areas. There is a place for adult poetry in the child's enjoyment, but not in lieu of that which speaks to him now in his own terms.

Poetry for children ought to be evaluated under the same terms as is that for adults, that is, by people who know children as well as poetry. As people come to understand that there is subject matter more appropriate for children and that children bring an increasing but not fully developed maturity to poetry, perhaps the disagreements can be resolved.

Children's poetry is that to which children respond. As adults, we want to offer the best in poetry as well. Need we worry about for what audience the poet wrote the poem? Our concern is with the listening audience of today.

Any book of poetry, then, becomes fair game for the person seeking poems for children. Certainly, not all will yield results, but one will never know until he has looked. In some cases, one will even find *parts* of poems that stand up well on their own and that are true to the poet's intent.

Reading Poetry Aloud

Poetry is best when presented orally. One reads this in every book about poetry, and yet it is a statement that can't be overstressed. There are certain difficulties connected with reading poetry—unfamiliar words, unfamiliar combinations of words, definite rhythm, pauses, variation, stress, new thoughts and ideas. It is too much to expect a child to cope with all of these, to read without verbalizing (which we caution him against), to get the impact of the poem and still to enjoy it. It is like handing him five apples and insisting that he juggle them competently at first try. (The analogy holds to the extent that experience and motivation can make both jugglers and poetry readers.)

The mere realization that we need to read poetry to children is insufficient. We must read well, or else we may as well not read at all. Reading aloud is gloriously rewarding, but it requires skill and practice. A tape recorder is vital to this effort, and having a live listener would help.

It is advisable to read the chosen poem over to oneself in order to become more familiar and comfortable with it. A dictionary may be necessary. Then one can decide as to "how he thinks the poem means," (a John Ciardi phrase), and how this meaning is translated into the spoken art. Punctuation marks, the ends of lines, should be noticed. Where is the best place to pause? To drop the voice? Is there a need to vary speed?

Generally, it is best to read at a comfortable speaking rate. Most students probably already know if their normal rate is too fast or too slow. It is advisable to slow down to build suspense, to suggest slow-moving action, to give the listener a chance to react, and to provide contrast. Contrast may also be provided by reading faster. One can also speed up reading to stimulate excitement or to suggest movement. The rate of speed should be changed both to aid meaning and to add interest.

Changes in voice dynamics help to interpret a poem. A booming bell in a poem should get appropriate treatment, as should a poem which suggests whispering. Again, a change in volume may be used for contrast, particularly in a poem of some length.

Timing is always important in oral reading and is basic to the reading of poems. Through the oral reader's interpretation, the poem's rhythm is shared. The bane of poetry is the sing-song reader. One should be very wary about reading a poem that insists on coming out sing-songy; this may be more the fault of the poem than the reader.

Can one sense what effect the poet is trying to achieve? In Milne's "Buckingham Palace," the march rhythm is evident. A natural interpretation is to read the four-line stanzas in martial style, with the "Says Alice" at the end of each stanza being comparable to a halt command.

The poems of Sara Teasdale have a quiet feeling touched with a sense of awe. They ask to be read quietly and evenly to communicate vocally a sense of wonder.

John Ciardi's poems for children bring to mind "tripping-the-light-fantastic." Nonsensical, tongue in cheek, they need to be read accordingly.

Listening to Carl Sandburg, one can get some insight into reading Sandburg. The individual words seem to mean more than the rhythm, and the poet seems to be talking with the listener rather than reading poetry.

The effective use of the pause is vital to good oral reading, and yet people seem to fear pausing. A pause may be used to keep the sense of what is being said, like a cliff-hanger, a contrast, a respite, a chance to anticipate. In poetry, pausing helps one maintain the rhythm. As a rule, there will be some sort of a pause, however slight, at the end of each line. The length of pause will depend on the rhythm and the meaning, the latter sensed only somewhat more intuitively than the former. The pause may be no more than a catch of breath, or of several seconds in duration. (The quietness of the latter is what some readers seem to be unable to tolerate. Whatever dire action they expect to happen in the silence probably won't happen.)

Punctuation marks may signal pause, and they *may* indicate that the reader's voice should drop. He should not automatically drop his voice at the end of a poetry line. Often anything more than a very slight pause at the end of a line would break the flow of meaning.

What expression should be put into reading a poem? This is where some people err on the side of doing too much. What mood(s) should the reader try to capture, using the utterance of each word to do so? He should make full use of tone, pitch, emphasis, timing, and loudness to put life into the poem.

Obviously, oral interpretations of a particular poem will differ, simply because personal interpretations of what the poet is saying will differ. But reading a poem to children is not for the purpose of satisfying the ham in the reader or for self-glorification, but rather, to introduce a poet's work in as honest and meaningful a way as possible. One of the complaints against poetry has been that some teachers have read so theatrically that the results were only laughable. "That's corny!" is an evaluation we can't afford.

The poetry voice, then, can be overdone. If it serves to make one more aware of the speaker than what is spoken, if it makes poetry too far away from the real world, then the oral reading of poetry has been unsuccessful. And yet, there must be something special in the reading. The poetry reader's voice and manner should differ noticeably from that of the giver of spelling tests and oral directions. Just as a good storyteller draws listeners by means of his voice, so should the reader of poetry.

Of course, proper articulation is necessary. Most of us have tendencies toward verbal carelessness that need to be guarded against.

A well-read poem is a pleasure for all. The novice reader needs to work on the mechanics of poetry so that he develops increasing ease, skill, and effectiveness in bringing poetry to children. For most of us, it does take practice. The tape recorder offers the sometimes traumatic, always revealing, opportunity for self-evaluation. Helpful in other ways are the suggestions and encouragement of a listener who has a good ear and heart for poetry.

When to Use Poetry

When does the teacher use poetry with children? The answer should be *daily*. Of course he is not likely to have a formally planned presentation every day, but there is always time for a poem or two. He may go so far as to have a specific time each day when the children can count on his sharing a poem. This may serve, in effect, as an excellent unifying activity, something to be anticipated. If the teacher does a good job, children will soon be requesting poems and even volunteering to read them.[3]

Incidental Use of Poems

Poetry is so much drawn from and related to what's happening, it should not be limited to a regular time but, rather, should appear whenever appropriate. Here are some suggestions:

The class is grumpy, and the children aren't accomplishing anything. A nonsense poem or two may be read.

---

[3]This is not entirely desirable. Some of the requests are likely to be unsuitable for use, and then what does one do? A child reading poetry aloud is likely to need some help from the teacher in reading effectively. (And yet, what danger there could be in discouraging the child's enthusiasm!)

The children are bubbling over the sight of the first robin. Any of several robin poems in Arbuthnot's *Time for Poetry* may be introduced.

It's John's birthday today. It can be marked by reading a poem of his choice or by reading an appropriate selection from *Birthday Candles Burning Bright*.

New baby brother? Blake's "Infant Joy" from *Songs of Innocence*.

The children are excited about the high school band that played for the assembly today. Selections from Plotz' *Untune the Sky* may be read.

The latest space vehicle has just blasted off into space. May Swenson's "Southbound on the Freeway" (*Poems to Solve*), or David McCord's "Go Fly a Saucer" (*Imagination's Other Place*), give the point of view of the visitor to earth and have something to say about contemporary life.

Holidays, seasons, weather, current events (including those happening to the pupils), last night's TV special—all the happenings of everyday life may be responded to through poetry.

Relation of Poetry to Prose

The alert, knowledgeable teacher will see many opportunities to tie in poetry with other forms of literature. Ezra Jack Keats' *Whistle for Willie*, a picture book that children should not miss, is about the very true-to-life efforts of Peter to learn to whistle. What better opportunity for Frances Frost's "The Little Whistler," with its hero(ine) in the same struggle. On a somewhat deeper level, there is the poem by an eleven-year-old who remembers when he first learned to whistle. The only person who appreciated his efforts was an old man who also had missing front teeth. ("When I Learned to Whistle" from *Miracles*)

In *The Shadow Book*, author Beatrice Schenk de Regniers and photographer Isabel Gordon explore the activities of children who are playing with their shadows. An excellent story hour could incorporate this and some of the many poems about shadows. Robert Louis Stevenson's "My Shadow" is well known but shouldn't be slighted for this reason. In "Shadow Dance," (Ivy Eastwick), a child explores what he can do with his shadow. Walter de la Mare's "The Shadow," from *Bells and Grass*, describes the beauty of the shadow at night.

Our Veronica Goes to Petunia's Farm would be complemented by animal poems. Selections from *I Went to the Animal Fair* and the "Beneath Man's Wings" section of *Under the Tent of Sky* would be particularly good.

Eve Merriam's "A Number of Numbers" (in *Catch a Little Rhyme*) fits quite naturally with a counting book. It and *Brian Wildsmith's 1 2 3s* could make a particularly happy combination.

Daniel Boone's Echo and echo poems; *It's Like This, Cat* and poems by young adolescents; *Treasure Island* and "Fifteen Men on a Dead Man's Chest"; *The Hobbit* and some of *The Songs of Tom Bombadil;* dragons in folklore and dragons in poetry; a Chinese folktale and poems of China . . . the possibilities are limitless. This pairing of prose and poetic literature should be used so that the selections can complement each other, not to show off the teacher's ingenuity. It can be forced, and it can be overdone.

Poetry and the Curriculum

Subjects in the curriculum can be enhanced by the inclusion of the right poem at the right time. *A Book of Americans,* many of Sandburg's poems, and *America Forever New* are representative of books that could be used in social studies. Science? *Imagination's Other Place, Shoots of Green,* and parts of *Bridled with Rainbows.* Music? Practically any poetry book, but especially *An Inheritance of Poetry,* with its index of musical settings, as well as Tolkien's *The Road Goes Ever On* and Wilder's *Lullabies and Night Songs,* both of which have musical notation. Art? *Hailstones and Halibut Bones.* Physical education? *Sprints and Distances.* Language? Any good poetry book. See especially *Words, Words, Words.*

In addition to including poems with activities of the school day, time needs to be set aside for more systematic approaches to poetry. Such sessions ought to occur at least weekly. If the teacher really wants these sessions, time can be found for them. In schools where there is freedom and flexibility, there will be no trouble in making time available. In more rigid schools, the relation of poetry to all subject areas can be utilized as a means to arrange time. For example, part of the reading period can legitimately be used for poetry. Presentations such as the ones suggested for math on pages 75 and 81 could certainly replace that subject for one day.

It must be assumed, then, that time and materials are available for a poetry program. How will one find the poems he wants to use for specific circumstances? A teacher's own collection of poems will provide for some occasions. His growing familiarity with materials will suggest useful sources. To find poems in a library collection, there are indexes to poetry which are most helpful.

Poetry Indexes — Finding a Particular Poem

BREWTON, JOHN and SARA. *Index to Children's Poetry;* A Title, Subject, Author, and First Line Index to Poetry in Collections for Children and Youth. New York: H. W. Wilson Co., 1942. (Indexes 130 collections.)

————. *Index to Children's Poetry.* 1st sup. New York: H. W. Wilson Co., 1957. (Indexes 66 collections.)

————. *Index to Children's Poetry.* 2d sup. New York: H. W. Wilson Co., 1965. (Indexes 85 collections.)

These indexes do for a group of poetry books what the index(es) does in a single poetry book, and more: they tell where to find a particular poem. A poet, the title of a poem, the first line of a poem can be looked up. If a poem for a particular setting is wanted, the subject can be looked up. The Brewtons list by symbol all books they have analyzed in which the poem is found. These symbols are decoded in the bibliography in the front of the book.

The good media specialist will check the list of collections indexed against the library holdings, and write down the call numbers for those which the library owns. Then all that is necessary is to go to the shelf to see if the book is in and if so, whether or not it is the one wanted. (The titles analyzed by the Brewtons may also be used as a guide in selecting poetry books to purchase.)

SELL, VIOLET et al., comp. *Subject Index to Poetry for Children and Young People.* Chicago: American Library Association, 1957. (157 titles indexed.)

Neither as comprehensive nor as up-to-date as the Brewton volumes, it does include page numbers for the poems. Some form headings are used, (e.g. ballads).

Using a poetry index can be a horrifying experience the first few times, but if it is backed up by a good book collection, it can be most helpful. When the number of books is limited, one might be better off checking each title for what is wanted.[4] It is hoped that eventually poetry indexes will include recorded poetry readings.

Poetry Sessions

Many formal poetry sessions are vital to a program. Some of these will be presentations of poetry on the part of a teacher, who chooses poetry around a particular theme. Some productive themes would be: Spring Poems, Just for Boys, Travel, People, (or Presidents or Abraham Lincoln), Colors, Playing, Families, Old Favorites, Poems for You, New Poems, Thanksgiving, The City. Several sources could be used to get variety and to introduce children to more than one book. Some samples

---

[4]A comprehensive source that the person making a very serious study of poetry should know is: John Mackay Shaw, *Childhood in Poetry*; A Catalogue, with biographical and critical annotations of the books of English and American poets comprising the Shaw *Childhood in Poetry* collections in the library of The Florida State University, with lists of the poems that relate to childhood, notes, and index by John Mackay Shaw (Detroit: Gale Research Company, 1967). 5 vol.

follow. Dialogue of the type that might be used is included to make the examples more concrete. Of course, everyone will present in his own style. Such presentations aim to provide an enjoyment of poetry and to give some idea of what poetry is. Questions are asked, comments encouraged, but these are certainly not lessons.

Facilitating Discussion

A word here about questioning technique. The discussion activities suggested are for the classroom in which children feel free to respond frankly. Questions are asked to stimulate thought, not to test memory. Too easily answered "yes" and "no" questions are avoided. The leader does not ask a question for the purpose of having the child parrot what he's supposed to say, but rather to get children to think and to share ideas. Open-ended questions for which there is rarely one "right" answer are asked. Interaction is encouraged, with the children questioning and commenting to each other. Communication is real, not superficial. Children are involved and really care about what they are saying and hearing; they don't merely assume roles. All answers are initially acceptable. It is the group, not the teacher, who disagrees. Creativity, thoughtfulness, and honesty of expression are prized.

The leader keeps things going, asking further appropriate questions as they arise from the discussion. He acts as a facilitator of communication.

The traditional view of the teacher as the ultimate authority so permeates schools that few children are able to avoid endowing the teacher's words with undue weight; to disagree would be unthinkable. Until children are able to accept the teacher's contribution as they do the contributions of others, the teacher should play an extremely limited role as discussion participant.

The wording of questions is vital to open discussion. Some typical questions follow, with suggestions on improving them:

Was that a nice thing for Janet to do? (Not only the wording, but the voice in which it is asked load the question. Better: What did you think of Janet's behavior? Would you have done what Janet did?)

What happened to Pablo in the poem? (How did you feel about what happened to Pablo?)

How many lines are there in this poem? (What do you notice about the structure of this poem?)

Define poetry. (What are some things you have discovered about poems?)

Was that a good choice of words used to describe the dog? (What words would you have used? What picture is drawn in your mind of the dog?)

Who wrote this poem? (What do you think you know about the author of this poem?)

Good discussion requires well-worded, thought- and feeling-provoking questions and an openness to responses. It is exciting, stimulating, often fatiguing, critical, and creative. Any activities that call for discussion are based on this kind of approach.

In groups where such openness is encouraged, children are likely to initiate discussion and to comment freely on what is presented.

Poetry on a Theme

At the beginning of the year, a teacher would probably be wise to prepare a general presentation similar to this. Such an approach can be successful even if he doesn't as yet know the children.

"Today I've brought a lot of poetry books from the library, and I'd like to share some with you. But before I start, I'd like to know what you thought when you heard me say the word, poetry?" (All answers should be accepted, even the hostile ones. Those that are negative at least help clear the air.)

"Here's a collection of poems I can almost guarantee that you'll like, beginning with the title, *Beastly Boys and Ghastly Girls*. William Cole collected these poems and then wrote this introduction." (The introduction is then read. This very non-prissy, nobody-should-be-good-all-the-time collection with its nasty children has never failed to delight groups of youngsters.)

"The verses are divided into sections like 'Never Stew Your Sister,' 'Wriggling, Giggling, Noise and Tattling,' 'The Naughtiest Children I Know,' and 'Beat Him when He Sneezes.'" (Several of the poems are then read.)

"Those poems are modern. Here's a book that has some old rhymes; you may already know some of them." (*Rocket in My Pocket*, compiled by Carl Withers. Two or three poems can be read, including a riddle or a spelling rhyme.)

"There are lots of poems for fun, as well as other kinds you'd like. What do you notice about these poems?" ("The Morning that Seemed Like Forever" and "Candy or Canary?" from Neville's *Woody and Me* can be read. Responses should indicate that the poems do not rhyme and that they are about everyday real life. The teacher should be prepared to accept more observations from the children than he has made himself.)

"Some poems make you think of noise." ("Tearing Around" from Neville's *Woody and Me*, "Bam, Bam, Bam" from Merriam's *Catch a Little Rhyme*, and "The Most of Being a Boy" from Ciardi's *The Man Who Sang the Sillies* can be read.)

"How is this next poem different?" (Then "Meeting" from Field's *Taxis and Toadstools,* a quiet and introspective poem, can be read.)

"To finish, here are some more light-hearted poems. This first man doesn't feel lighthearted, but I do." (The teacher can read the title poem from Doob's *A Crocodile Has Me by the Leg,* "Rolling Stones" from Aileen Fisher's *Runny Days, Sunny Days,* and the title poem from William Jay Smith's *Laughing Time.*)

(If the children are alert and interested, "Laughing Time" could be rather easily worked out for choral speaking. At all times, the teacher should be aware of the class. If they are responding well, additional poems from these books may be used. On the other hand, the pupils may be too restless for so many. Good discussion or serendipitous happenings should be capitalized on.)

This session was planned with involvement of children at various times primarily to increase their awareness of poetry, but also to keep their interest and attention. Humorous poems were used initially because of their appeal to children; then some poems of greater depth were read, followed by the reading of more humorous poems for the sole purpose of relaxation. It is a good idea always to make immediately available to the children the poetry books that have been used and others they might enjoy, as well as poetry recordings for those who might find pleasure in this approach. After the first session, these books, plus additional titles by Ciardi, Smith, and Merriam, and recordings by Ciardi should be handy, as should several good anthologies, such as *American Mother Goose* and Lear's *Complete Nonsense Book.*

With young children, such sessions will be quite short. Initially, just a few simple rhymes would be shared. Sessions may be lengthened gradually, and increasingly difficult poems may be included. Because the attention span of children is brief, it is particularly important to involve them directly in the poems. Using finger plays, dramatizing the rhymes, reciting a poem with the teacher, singing along, all are easy and obvious ways for young children to participate. They delight in being taught a new rhyme—once or twice through it by the teacher and the children are ready to join in.

Even kindergarteners will arrive at the place where they enjoy presentations such as the following one on pets.

"If you had your choice of pets, what would you ask for?" (The teacher might write down who says what, so that he can acknowledge their responses.) "What do you notice about your choices?"

"Here are some poems about pets, and many of them are about pets you have mentioned." (The well-prepared teacher will have lots of poems ready and marked, and will play much of this session by ear. The following poems were selected for variety in content and approach.

Several are not particularly simple, but are included for the responsive child, and to help the whole group "stretch.")

PETS

"Birthday Present" from Fisher's *Cricket in a Thicket*. (Any kind of dog will do.)

"My Puppy" from Fisher's *Runny Days, Sunny Days*.

"The Bath" from Moore's *Cinnamon Seed*. (A bath is very hard on cats, because they do not like water.)

"The Turtle" from Moore's *Cinnamon Seed*.

"The Goldfish" from Moore's *Cinnamon Seed*. (A mysterious, lovely poem.)

"No Man Exists" from *A Crocodile Has Me by the Leg*. (Some animals will never be anyone's pet!)

"Open House" from Fisher's *In the Woods, in the Meadows, in the Sky*. (A child imagines what animals he'd want living with him if he were a tree.)

"Mick" from Reeves' *The Blackbird in the Lilac*. (The beloved mongrel.)

"Radiator Lions" from Aldis' *All Together*. (The child who can't have a pet. Some children may be unfamiliar with this type of radiator.)

MATHEMATICS

"There Was an Old Man Who Said, Do," from *Rainbow in the Sky*, edited by Louis Untermeyer. (Limerick about addition.)

"Arithmetic" from Carl Sandburg's *Wind Song*.

"Numbers" from Aliki Barnstone's *The Real Tin Flower*.

"As I Was Going to St. Ives." (Traditional riddle.)

"Hall and Knight or $z + b + x = y + b + z$" from Rieu's *The Flattered Flying Fish*.

"Equations" from Hubbell's *Catch Me a Wind*.

"Gazinta" from Merriam's *It Doesn't Always Have to Rhyme*.

"Jonathan Bing Does Arithmetic" by Beatrice Curtis Brown. Found in Brewton's *Gaily We Parade*.

"Multiplication Is Vexation," from Mother Goose. Found in Brewton's *Bridled with Rainbows*.

DINOSAURS

"Long Gone" from Prelutsky's *A Gopher in the Garden*.

"When Dinosaurs Ruled the Earth" from Hubbell's *The Apple Vendor's Fair*.

Several selections can be read, depending upon time and interest, from Richard Armour's *A Dozen Dinosaurs*.

"The Dinosaur" by Bert Leston Taylor. Found in Plotz' *Imagination's Other Place*.

"Steam Shovel" by Charles Malam. Found in Dunning's *Reflections on a Gift of Watermelon Pickle*.

TODAY

"Automation" from Hubbell's *Catch Me a Wind*.

"Sky's Nice" from Johnson's *Feather in My Hand*. (Flying in an airplane.)

"Fishing Trip" from Johnson's *Feather in My Hand*.

"Banjo Scott" from Starbird's *The Pheasant on Route Seven*. (A sympathetic view of the town drunk.)

"Beatle Dream" from Barnstone's *The Real Tin Flower*.

"The Toll Taker" from Hubbell's *The Apple Vendor's Fair*.

"Three Minutes" from Neville's *Woody and Me* (The book report.)

"The Army Horse and the Army Jeep" from Ciardi's *The Reason for the Pelican*.

SO YOU DON'T LIKE POETRY

These were chosen to include humor, variety in poetry, fun with words, masculine flavor in poetry, and thoughtful poetry. There are far too many for a single session. The aim is to reopen the world of poetry for those who have lost interest, or worse, those who never did like poetry.

"The Corps of Discovery" from Daugherty's *West of Boston*. (Lewis and Clark expedition.)

"Jeremi and Josephine" from Richards' *Tirra Lirra*. (Reminiscent of *Mad Libs* in that the reader can fill in the blanks himself.)

"Mean Song" from Merriam's *There Is No Rhyme for Silver*. (Dire threats in made-up words; compare to "Jabberwocky.")

"Zero Weather" from Fisher's *Runny Days, Sunny Days*. (Short poem with good use of imagery.)

"This Is My Rock" from McCord's *Far and Few*. (One's special place to be alone.)

"Minnie Morse" from Starbird's *Don't Ever Cross a Crocodile*. (The ubiquitous horsey girl.)

"Song of an Unlucky Man" from *A Crocodile Has Me by the Leg*, edited by Leonard Doob. (Ruefully funny, unrhymed poem of another culture.)

"Goose, Moose & Spruce" from McCord's *Take Sky*. (Vagaries of English plurals.)

"Time Leaves No Time when You're a Boy" from Ciardi's *The Monster Den*.

"Dreams" from Hughes' *The Dream Keeper.* (A short poem of a very different flavor, challenging and capable of really moving some listeners.)

"Solomon Grundy" from Mother Goose, and then the parody of it in Winsor's *The Space Child's Mother Goose.*

"Santa Fe West" from Behn's *The Golden Hive.* (Modern life.)

"The Morning that Seemed Like Forever" from Neville's *Woody and Me.* (Disgusted view of a day, with unglorified everyday life.)

Poetry Book Talk

Occasionally, the teacher may want to introduce his class to a particular book of poetry. He may show the book, discuss its table of contents, and then read some of the poems. Perhaps he can read from the introduction. This may be a good time to introduce the idea of using the table of contents and index(es) to find something specific.

The book talk is an excellent technique for a teacher to use to introduce children to a group of books in such a way as to entice them into choosing books to read from his suggestions. A poetry book talk might be done very effectively. This emphasis on the child's reading to himself means that it is rather unlikely that the poetry book talk technique will be used until at least third grade or later. It is advisable that the teacher have a unifying theme of some sort as a basis for his choice. The reader might find it interesting to try to determine the theme for the following book talk.

"Here's an old book of poetry that I found in another library." (The teacher reads a poem or two and shows the format.) "How does this compare to the poetry books in our library?

"Do you remember *Brian Wildsmith's ABC's?* The fable books he illustrated? Did you know that he also illustrated a poetry book? It's called *The Oxford Book of Poetry for Children.* Here are some of his pictures." (He shows the pictures and reads some of the poems accompanying them.) "The cover of this book is purple, unlike very many other books. The title is stamped on in gold. Why might these colors have been chosen?

"This book is quite different, even from the outside." (Much taller, thinner. He shows *Beyond the High Hills.*) "There are at least two things about it that are unusual for a poetry book." (He reads several poems, shows the photographs, and encourages the children to feel free to ask for the poem if they like the photograph.) "What kind of person do you think wrote these poems?" (Discussion of traditional literature, which leads into the next title.)

"What did you find special about *Beyond the High Hills?*" (All comments should be accepted, but the teacher should make certain that the ideas of the use of color photography and the fact that these are all traditional Eskimo poems, are mentioned.)

"This book also uses photographs, but they are not in color, and they could have been taken in many places. These poems are modern —we know the poets and have an idea when they wrote." (*Reflections on a Gift of Watermelon Pickle*. The teacher reads "Crossing Kansas by Train" by Donald Justice, "Some Brown Sparrows" by Bruce Fearing, and Arthur Guiterman's "On the Vanity of Earthly Greatness." He shows the picture on page 26 and asks the children to guess what is being shown. Then he introduces a recording of the poems.)

"Perhaps you've already discovered *Creatures Great and Small*. This is a book of animal poems, each with its own illustrations. Here are several of my favorites." (He reads "The Giraffe" and "The Walrus" and shows pictures of these and others. He responds to one or two requests.)

"Remember David McCord? I've read from his books before. Here's a new book with some of the old poems illustrated in color. Mr. McCord writes different kinds of poems. We have a record of him reading his own poems, and so I'll play parts of that and show you the pictures from *Every Time I Climb a Tree*." (The teacher plays the title poem, "Pad and Pencil," and "Crows.")

"All of these books are here for you to borrow. Do you know why I chose these particular titles? I thought you'd enjoy the poems, and I also thought you'd enjoy the books themselves. Poetry books are getting better and better to look at, as you can see. There are some other attractive books I didn't mention that you may want to look at." (A good collection to have on hand would include Lewis' *In a Spring Garden, The Wind and the Rain, Miracles,* and *Out of the Earth I Sing*; also *The Christopher Robin Book of Verse, Feather in My Hand, A Gopher in the Garden,* and *Cats and Bats and Things with Wings*. The children should be given time to enjoy them.)

Discovering Poets

Another approach to poetry is to introduce a poet and his works. Biographical information, books of his writings, as well as single poems from anthologies can be assembled. To make the person more real, the teacher might try to find photographs of him and recordings of his voice. The length and depth of the study will be determined by children's interest, the materials available, and the significance of the poet. Children may become interested in learning about poets on their own. (But the mass assignment, with each child doing a poet, should be avoided. Even if there were enough materials to make such an activity practical, the net effect could be to kill interest.)

Some useful sources for biographical information are:

Single biographies of the poet, for example, James Playsted Wood's *The Snark Was a Boojum,* a life of Lewis Carroll, and Sandburg's autobiography, *Always the Young Strangers.*

Collective biographies, for example, Charlemae Rollins' *Famous American Negro Poets.*

Names of poets can be looked up in the card catalog, indexes to selection sources, periodical indexes such as *Library Literature* and *Education Index. Elementary English* and *Horn Book* may be the most helpful magazine sources.

Someone has suggested that this approach can become a study of a poet and not of his work. Wisely managed, a biographical study should make a poet's work more meaningful, because a background has now been established, and this should make him seem like more of a person to the children.

Forms of Poetry

The teacher may devote some sessions to exploring forms of poetry, for example, haiku and/or ballads.

"The Japanese people have a kind of poetry with which Americans are just becoming acquainted. It's called haiku poetry.

"*In a Spring Garden* is one of the best poetry books to look at that I know." (The teacher reads three or four haiku that he particularly likes, and shows the pictures, or uses the filmstrip and record.)

"Here are some haiku for you to read." (It is preferable to prepare transparency [ies] for overhead projection, or to use the blackboard, but ditto or mimeo reproduction would work.) "What do you notice about haiku?" (Children will notice qualities of form and content. The teacher reads more as the children show a desire to hear more haiku. Lewis' *Moment of Wonder* and Behn's *Cricket Songs* can be used, and illustrations which are reproductions of Japanese art can be shown. This would be a wonderful opportunity to tie together art and poetry by bringing other Japanese art into the classroom. Given opportunity, encouragement, and time, children can discover the "haikuness" of haiku. The leader must give them enough haiku from which they can generalize, and he should perhaps ask less broad questions so as not to force the issue.)

"Americans are now trying to write haiku. Harry Behn, who translated *Cricket Songs,* wrote these." (He reads "From an Airplane" in *The Golden Hive* and "Haiku for a Week in Spring" from Hubbell's *Catch Me a Wind.*) "How do these compare to Japanese haiku? How might you illustrate them?" (This may make the presentation too long or purposeful. An enjoyment of and a desire to get acquainted with more haiku are the most important outcomes. Certainly, illustrations and/or writing of haiku could be very logical activities.)

A variety of ballads can be presented by the teacher, among them: "Get Up and Bar the Door" (humorous);

"Ballad of Robin Hood" (Exquisitely detailed illustrations can be shown on the opaque projector. It might be fun to sing one of the ballads, reading some of the verses for contrast. Hero story.);

"The Farmer's Curst Wife" from Adshead's *An Inheritance of Poetry*; and

"Lord Randal" (tragedy).

(A recording of a modern ballad that is popular at the moment can be played; this will show the continuing life of this form. Some junior high teachers start with the words of today's pop music, because they find them not only relevant to the pupils and thus a key to developing interest, but also often poetic.)

Audiovisual Materials and Poetry

Poetry sessions should include audiovisual materials. Some children will never get to the actual reading of poetry themselves. For them, the availability of poetry in non-print forms may be the only way in which they will (can?) accept poetry.

For all of us, the variety offered by non-print media is a consideration, as is the effectiveness of using them. Television, movies, radio, record players, and tape recorders are so much a part of modern life that to reject their use would be naive. The possibilities for what can be done with poetry are greatly extended by using mechanical means. The sound of other voices, musical accompaniment, visualization, movement, size, and professionalism are factors encouraging use of these media.

One of the most cogent arguments for the use of audiovisual materials is their repeatability. A record can be played, or a film viewed whenever equipment and time are available. The non-reader doesn't need to have an adult present in order to enjoy Walter de la Mare's work or a poem like "Casey at the Bat" when these selections are recorded for the child's use.

Sometimes audiovisual materials may be used to set the stage for poetry: pictures of Robert Frost's New England; an aerial view to gain perspective for Behn's "From an Airplane," or a recording of a train in transit for his "Lost" (both from *The Golden Hive*); cloud forms; animal pictures and sounds; music of various moods; pictures of people in *A Book of Americans;* art both flat and three-dimensional; or a film about African tribal life to introduce primitive African poetry. A slide of the Changing of the Guard invites one to share Milne's "They're Changing the Guard at Buckingham Palace." Children might touch and feel certain materials that suggest poems.

There is a growing number of recorded poetry readings for children, readings which are very well done. Many have a poet reading his own work. Others alternate the use of male and female voices to good effect. Some have musical background, or the reader sings part of the time.

However, many poetry records do not lend themselves well to a class presentation. They don't involve the listener enough, or they lack general interest. Warmth may be missing. It would be well to identify those records to which classes do respond and those from which a short segment can be played effectively. Some records are highly successful with the individual listener, and some (however bad we may feel about this) will find no audience. And the only way to find out is to *try*. A mother recently dismissed two poetry records as having absolutely no child appeal—until she found her third-grader listening intently to all four sides.

One weakness noticeable in available recordings is that many modern poems are not recorded. This is probably due to problems in getting permission to reproduce an author's work. Since the spoken poetry just might lead to the book, this embargo seems unfortunate for the publisher as well as for the would-be user whose listening is unnecessarily limited.

In John Ciardi's recording of *I Met a Man*, he talks to the audience as if he were in the room with them, and they respond accordingly. The Caedmon *Mother Goose* record has children singing along, clapping, bouncing, grinning, and oohing with no more invitation than its own exuberance.

Several recording companies are doing notable work with poetry for children. One would do well to write for their catalogs:

Folkways/Scholastic Records   Spoken Arts, Inc.
906 Sylvan Avenue   59 Locust Avenue
Englewood Cliffs, N. J. 07632   New Rochelle, N. Y. 10801

Caedmon Records   Pathways of Sound
508 8th Avenue   102 Mt. Auburn St.
New York, N. Y. 10018   Cambridge, Massachusetts

CMS Records, Inc.
14 Warren Street
New York, N. Y. 10007

Filmstrips and films are just beginning to be produced for poetry. Weston Woods Studio (Weston, Connecticut) has added poetry to their visual reproductions, with such titles as "Casey at the Bat," "In a Spring Garden," and "The Owl and the Pussycat." Several films have been made by using the iconographic technique in which illustrations from the books of the same name are photographed for projection.

Several films are concerned with motivating children to write poetry.

A most stimulating film has been made from Mary O'Neill's *Hailstones and Halibut Bones*. An imaginative cartooning technique shows one person's interpretation of six of the colors in the book. The effect is nearly psychedelic. Arguments rage fiercely over usage—some would use the film at every opportunity, some would show the pictures, others would use only the sound track. The subject and treatment are such that the film, as is the case with the book, has wide appeal.

Flat pictures, art reproductions, and slides may be used to complement poetry. The adult's alertness and ingenuity will determine the usefulness of the pictorial approach. Little has been done by commercial companies. Transparencies to be used on the overhead projector likewise have great possibilities for poetry, but the teacher will probably have to develop his own.

The concept of teacher-made materials is far from new. But there is an increasing trend toward teachers making more sophisticated materials, using photography and sound-recording. The latter is simple and has great usefulness in the poetry program. The teacher can record listening experiences for children, to be available at all times. He can use the voices of others, sound effects, and musical accompaniment. With experience, a course in the preparation of media, and/or expert guidance, he can use photography for still and moving pictures. Techniques for transparency-making can produce surprisingly effective visuals.

There are exciting possibilities for the use of realia and other three-dimensional objects in a poetry program. Stones or shells which the children handle and describe can be an excellent introduction or follow-up to appropriate poems. Musical instruments, Christmas decorations, models, globes, and textiles are some of the stimuli that might be used.

Audiovisual materials should be used only if they have something to contribute, and not as an attempt to kill time or to be modern. Their use requires skill in presentation, a fact that is far more important than the rather simple technical skills needed in operating equipment.

For the McLuhan age, one must turn to electronic modes of presentation. And yet the danger of so packaging materials that nothing is left for the child to imagine or think must be reiterated. Carefully chosen materials, imaginatively presented and not overused, have much to offer the poetry program. (See Selected References in Chapter 2, Part II-D.)

Children Read Poetry

So far, the suggestions have centered in the presentation of poems to children. This may be the most effective way to present poetry well and to reach most children. Care should be taken that this procedure not become too passive. An enthusiastic teacher who is responsive to his pupils and who actively involves them through questioning and comments, need have no fears of passivity.

Our aim, that children learn to love poetry, goes beyond the classroom and the present. Children need to be encouraged to read poetry to themselves, to each other, and to us.

This means materials easily accessible—some short, some simple, some comprehensive, some specialized, and all potentially appealing.

It means time for children to read poetry. After some poetry sessions, the teacher will want to have a reading time. For the youngest, this may consist of time to browse through Mother Goose books and illustrated books of poems. Children could recite many of the nursery rhymes to each other. The teacher would circulate among the pupils and read to them.

It is doubtful that there will ever be a day when every child in a class will want to and be able to read poetry. But by the time that there are many attractive books from which to choose, as well as the option of listening to or viewing poetry, most children will make good use of time allowed for personal enjoyment of poetry. By adding possibilities for creative activities stemming from poetry, every child should find something appealing to him.

Sometimes it is a good idea to give older children the freedom to read poetry in groups. Their varying interests, enthusiasms, and reading abilities will interact upon each other, and the experience will be fuller than any they would have had alone.

Poetry reading/viewing/listening on an individual basis ought always to be encouraged. Children should be able to check out and take home any materials in which they are interested, even to the projector needed for viewing.

They should have opportunities to share poetry orally with others if they'd like to. Until they can do this comfortably and fairly well, however, their reading to a group should not be encouraged.

The teacher will probably need to have some class sessions on effective reading of poetry. (He should avoid overdoing in this area, however, lest the children emerge bored or hypercritical.) For example, a poem might be projected by means of a transparency. The children would be asked to read it silently. The teacher gives help with the words, but does not read the poem aloud. He asks questions such as: "How does this poem make you feel?" "What mood does the poet set?" "How would you read this poem?" "Would you read it all in the same way?"

It seems appropriate to suggest that the reader who wants to make his audience really care tries to read in such a way that the poem comes alive for them. In some classes, children could suggest many techniques for oral reading of poems from their own experience. With other groups, the teacher may need to provide some of the information with which they could work.

He could have a number of children read the same lines in different ways and see which oral interpretations seem to fit well. (There is no absolute best way!)

Or he could provide bad examples and ask: "How could this reading be improved? Try reading it your way." A good reading might elicit suggestions as to what made it successful. Two people could read the same poem differently and then discuss why they may have read as they did. Their techniques may be compared and their effectiveness evaluated. Not only could such an approach help the child reader, but it ought to help him develop into a more appreciative listener.

Choral Speaking

A popular and effective means of using poetry orally is through choral speech. If the teacher has been associated with a singing choir, he should have an excellent background for the transition to speech choir work. Each has a director, but good training, experience, and group rapport may eventually cut down on the need for a director. The music director's job is to choose appropriate materials and introduce them to the group in a meaningful way. He works to get voices in the group to blend harmoniously. He marks rhythm so that the group will stay together. He uses differences in volume and timing to interpret the meaning of the music; he emphasizes diction to make the words understandable. Entrances and cutoffs are directed to make a disciplined effect. And he tries to make the whole process enjoyable to the participants while adding to their knowledge of music.

In choral speaking, the primary difference is that the director gives the choir increasing opportunities to help in planning the interpretation. The only score needed is a poem, and accompaniment is not a consideration.

Actually, choral speaking is not limited to poetry, but they go together beautifully, and poems are probably the best source for the speech choir.

Why use choral reading of poetry? Primarily, because it adds to children's enjoyment of poetry by directly involving them in it. They gain ease in the reading of poetry and greater skill in its oral interpretation. Hopefully, the amount of time spent on a poem used will make it more meaningful.

As a speech activity, choral speaking is excellent for developing group cooperation and rapport. Everyone is a contributor to the group; here is a place where equality can become reality. The shy child participates fully, and he is frequently found volunteering for a solo part.

The first step is selecting the poetry—poems with high appeal, those that read aloud particularly well, those which would lend themselves to the use of a group of voices, those which have a melodic sound, a flowing rhythm. Probably, a skilled director and an experienced choir can effectively do almost any poem. However, a few poems seem just too personal to involve a group. Others which are so even in meter that they can hardly avoid monotony should be avoided, at least until the group is skilled. The teacher is urged to choose poems that are worth spending time on. In the course of a year, he should be sure to choose a good variety of poems. Certainly, children should be involved in the selection process.

Getting started when one has never tried choral speaking is the most fearsome part. The biggest help to a novice is to tell himself emphatically that he is the director and, therefore, must direct the rhythm, dynamics, attacks, and cutoffs. The children must be trained from the start to look at him for direction. This is a group effort, not just a number of individuals each going his own way. There must be a unifying force, and that force is the director.

It is advisable to start with simple materials. A well-known rhyme can be chosen for the pupils to say together. Their first efforts, which are not directed, should be tape-recorded. After the tape is played back, the teacher asks what was good, and what could be improved. Children are very likely to pinpoint most of the difficulties. Their suggestions should be tried out, but with the teacher assuming the direction of the choral reading this time through.

The problem in group work is that it is easy for it to become terribly amorphous. Dragging speed (ever sing around a campfire?), sing-song rhythm, monotone sound, and sloppy unison are some of the most glaring weaknesses.

The children need to know what the director is working toward—specifically, a group sound which is as pleasing to listen to as a single voice, but which is able to do more. Recordings of good examples of choral speech, or even better, a live group that can present a desirable model, should be most helpful. After that, it is up to the director.

Poems with repetition are easy to start on. A refrain can easily be taught to the class, then polished, and the verses read by solo voices (or perhaps by the director initially). One teacher tells of using the lyrics of folksongs to start his secondary school students speaking chorally.[5] Other poems are like litanies, and the class can do the response

---

[5]William Cullen, "The First Thirty Minutes of Choral Reading," *English Journal* 57 (March 1968), 395-399+.

while individual voices read the different lines. Examples are "The Circus Is Coming to Town" and "Names" from the Prologue to Carl Sandburg's "The Family of Man" (found in *Wind Song*). "Old Snake Has Gone to Sleep" from *Nibble Nibble* by Margaret Wise Brown offers the same form with contrasting subject matter.

This kind of approach can illustrate both the problems and the joys of poetry. With so much repetition, one can all too quickly settle into a deadening pattern of dum de dum de dum de dum. On the other hand, if the teacher explores what can be done to vary and brighten a repeated line, he can quickly establish the essence of good choral speaking.

Starting with materials children already know or can learn easily has the advantage of making their total attention available to the director. This way they can get used to following a director.

The unison is really the most difficult kind of choral work that can be done, both in music and in speech. To divide voices is somewhat easier and increases the effects that can be achieved. For some poems, it is sufficient to divide the group as they are sitting, but much of the time, the teacher will want to group children according to their normal speaking pitch.

Voices can simply alternate verses. Usually, it is advisable to use the meaning of the poem as a basis for dividing parts. Poems with contrast, question and answer, a natural alternation, lend themselves to two voices.

"Rebellion in September" (from *Poems* by Rachel Field) is an invitation to two-part work. In the poem, the child is having trouble adjusting to the inside school world when the out-of-doors is so inviting. His scholarly questions are printed in italics, while the regular print states the thoughts that really concern him.

Because each line expresses a complete thought, this poem from Christina Rossetti's *Sing-Song* could be used with two groups (or more) alternating the lines.

> A pin has a head, but has no hair;
> A clock has a face, but no mouth there;
> Needles have eyes, but they cannot see;
> A fly has a trunk without lock or key;
> A timepiece may lose, but cannot win;
> A cornfield dimples without a chin;
> A hill has no leg, but has a foot;
> A wine glass a stem, but not a root;
> A watch has hands, but no thumb or finger;
> A boot has a tongue, but is no singer;
> Rivers run, though they have no feet;
> A saw has teeth, but it does not eat;
> Ash trees have keys, yet never a lock;
> And baby crows, without being a cock.

"Where Is a Poem" (Eve Merriam, *There Is No Rhyme for Silver*) has an interesting structure of three stanzas. The first has five lines. A second group could read the second stanza, which has six lines. The last stanza is rather long and is made up of rhyming couplets. The beginning and ending couplets might best be done in unison, but the rest could be alternated between two groups.

James Reeves' *Wandering Moon* includes a poem called "The Sea," which compares the sea to a dog. The first stanza could be spoken by the whole group. The second emphasizes the loudness and the activity of the sea; heavy voices should read this. In the last stanza, lighter voices can interpret the sea at rest.

Using three voice groups can make a still more interesting reading. High voices can suggest lightness, excitement, femininity, frivolity, youth. Medium voices are down-to-earth, can provide the ongoing narration, sound easygoing. The lower voices sound masculine, solid, gruff, even fearsome.

The use of unison and any combination of groups and solo voices can further widen the possibilities for interpretation of poetry.

How are voices divided? They are divided on the basis of their natural speaking pitch. Older children may be asked to divide themselves on the basis of whether they think their voices are high, medium, or low, since most of them will judge rightly. Then each group speaks a sentence or rhyme together, and the teacher can change those whose voices don't blend. With younger children, the teacher sorts them and then checks the sound.

Some people suggest that voice quality need not be used as a basis for division, but that children can be divided into groups arbitrarily. However, the effect that can be obtained by the use of similar voices justifies the slight effort entailed in setting up voice groups.

As the teacher presents a poem for choral speaking, he reads the poem and talks about it. (He must be careful not to lecture but to discuss the poem openly.) He must be sure that the children can understand the poem well enough to be able to get involved in it, not just to mouth the words. He should never continue with a poem that obviously is unpopular with the children.

Before starting, the teacher should have a general idea as to how he thinks the poem should sound. He should give the children an increasingly greater share in planning the interpretation. When choral speaking is new, he will have to introduce them to the potential of voice choirs.

The teacher will need to consider which voices will read what parts. What will be the normal speed at which the poem is read? Where and how will he vary from it? What changes in loudness will he make, and where? What expression will he use? Voice inflection? Where will the pauses come?

All children should be watching the director when it is time to start. Each voice group is seated in a designated area. The children either know the poem by heart or they can see it easily. A transparency projected on the overhead may be the best way for all to see and also to have their attention focused. It is important to make sure that, from the beginning, the children speak with meaning so that they fall into the habit of working as a disciplined group.

One reason for using a simple start is that children need to get used to hand signals, and the director needs to get used to making them. He should let the children know what these signals are. Movements that he feels comfortable with and that convey meaning to the choir are quite good enough; a standardized technique for directing seems unnecessary.

A signal that the choral speaking is about to begin should be made so that the children are ready for direction. An opening of the hand can indicate that it's time to start, just as closing the hand indicates a cutoff. Simply pointing at the group can be an effective starter. Both of these should be fast and definite so that beginnings and endings are spared a ripple effect.

The director can beat the feet of the poem if he remembers that many of the feet will be irregular and if he can avoid the sing-song syndrome. A combination of this and word-by-word, as the context seems to indicate, may be best. Strict word-by-word direction gets a bit intense. Mouthing the words along with the children can be a great help in keeping them together, especially when getting started.

Loudness can be indicated by making larger directional movements, quietness by pulling back.

Directing expression is more difficult. Much of this will be done in planning with the group ahead of time. Facial expressions can help and so can movements. Such qualities as lightness, bounce, and ponderousness can be communicated by hands and arms.

The director can help children handle line endings by the relative position of his hand, showing whether the voices should go up, drop, or stay the same.

Above all, the leader and the group must feel the poem. Each time they hear it, it will become more a part of them and easier to do. They will see how they can improve the sound.

Poems and lines within a poem can be tried in various ways. Which sounds better? How does changing oral interpretation change meaning?

For better voice control and sound, the children should stand for at least part of the time.

How much time should be spent on a poem? For some, two or three times through would be plenty. For others, this would be only enough to give children the flavor. It is advisable to stop while interest is still high. Most poems will be used in more than one session anyway. Satisfaction with the rendition of the poem is far more important than achieving a perfectly polished production.

Most choral reading periods will be involved with more than one poem. Typically, the teacher will be introducing a new poem, working on several that have not reached acceptable standards, and doing some old favorites that children request.

The greatest dangers in voice choir work lie at opposite ends of the scale. Those who tolerate poor quality work are doing little more than marking time. The leader who gets overly engrossed in the product loses the children and the poem.

Wisely used, choral speaking is an activity that is stimulating, meaningful, and enjoyable to all. Occasionally, the work should be shared with an audience—with pupils in another classroom, with parents, or with a large group in the assembly hall.

There are books of poems which are scored for choral reading. The quality of verse, however, tends to be low. Part of this is due to the royalties asked by publishers and poets. But too much of it is because of the compilers' (oftentimes) ignorance of good poetry, as well as their primary concern for poems that lend themselves well to scoring, rather than a concern for the merit of the poem itself. In some cases, poetry is being used (misused) to teach speech sounds, or morality and etiquette. At any rate, even a good collection chosen for choral speech need not be any better than those poems the teacher can gather himself.

Chants make fine material for the choir. Books of primitive poetry will have particularly good selections, since many of the poems are what groups did say together. "Praise Song for a Drummer" from (Doob's *A Crocodile Has Me by the Leg*) is an excellent example. Sometimes, the rhymes and chants children themselves speak can be used. A kind of collage of traditional sayings could even be worked out.

The use of special effects seems unnecessary, although there are those who will use scenery and sound to augment their speech choir. In the writer's opinion, this smacks too much of showmanship, although occasional sparing use might not be harmful.

Choral speaking can add a new dimension to poetry. By directly involving children, by emphasizing meaning and its interpretation through speech, by acquainting children with lots of poems of high quality, by using the interest of the group to stimulate that of the individual, and by having something a group can proudly share with another, choral speaking adds significantly to the total poetry program.

Memorizing Poetry

One outcome of choral speaking is that children tend to memorize the poems with which they work. What about memorization? Arguments wax hot on its value, with the vast majority being against forced memorization.

Whatever the values of forced memorization may be, they don't seem to outweigh the disadvantages. Too many college students inveigh against memorization as being the greatest deterrent to true appreciation of poetry that ever was invented by man. The famed "thirty lines (more for extra credit)" make poetry a quantity and not a quality, a chore rather than a source of personal pleasure.

The drudgery of memorization is often heightened by the requirement to recite one's poem(s) in front of the class. When everyone painfully recites—and must listen to—the same selection, it is little wonder that pupils become poetry dropouts. What can be the objectives of teachers insisting on such assignments? (Perhaps an excellent way to drive out the cut-rate verse would be to force memorization of it and then provide lots of pleasant experiences with good poetry.)

Giving the child a choice of what he is to memorize seems little better. Many children will simply choose a poem that's easy and accessible in order to get it over with. Meaning? Who cares! Teacher said to memorize a poem and I will, so I can watch TV tonight!"

Rote memorization of any sort in schools today has become minimal. The alphabet seems to grow on children by virtue of their many experiences with it. Arithmetic facts are introduced through their meaning, and children are often allowed to solve problems by doing the computations in any way they can. Pupils are taught how to use reference books to find out populations, capitals, products, number of feet in a mile, and so forth. In science, children learn to work with method and materials. The message of the Gettysburg Address is more likely to be discussed than the words memorized. Meaning and methods are replacing memory; memorization is incidental rather than forced.

Memorization should be introduced to children as a way by which some people can enjoy poetry. The teacher, by being able himself to share poems from his memory, may encourage some children to learn their favorites by heart. But a child must never be required to memorize one word!

It seems that the time spent on memory work might better be spent listening to Harry Behn reading his poems, or leafing through *An Inheritance of Poetry,* or daydreaming about what May Swenson has wrapped up in her riddle poems.

Who speaks for memorization? Those who do seem to have two arguments. Some say that it is good discipline. One can only ask, For what? If the discipline justification is tracked down, it may turn out to mean that the supporter considers it part of our heritage. And what this really means is that "my teacher thought it was good for me, so it must be good for you, too."

In every college class, one or two people will say, "I had to memorize poems, and I'm happy to have these poems always ready. It pleases me to remember them and think of what they say." Others say, "I really resented memorizing them, but I'm glad now that I still remember those poems."

Here is the only real argument for memorization that seems acceptable. Poems that have something to say to us may continue to do so in time to come. Committed to memory, they are there when we want them. Memories of friends, places visited, art objects, things that have happened—all may serve to comfort and enrich our lives in just the same way.

Even here, there are reservations. How much of this pleasure in the known poem is nothing more than sentiment? (Two friends, years later, happily discover that they are able to recite a poem learned in grade school. Is it the poem that pleases them, or all the recollections that it calls up? Or is it pride in their memory?)

How often is it the full poem that we recall? More likely, it is a memorable phrase or verse. And aren't these poems that bring so much pleasure to us likely to be in our personal poetry collections anyway and therefore easy to get at most of the time?

One of the advocates for memorization of poetry is Padraic Colum, who says that it provides "mental and imaginative capital."[6] Because he speaks as a humanist and as a poet, his views should be read as a contrast to what most authorities are saying today.

The real objection to forced memorization is the insistence that a child memorize whether he wants to or not. Usually, there are further constraints put on him to make the assignment even less palatable. We know that the casualty rate on poetry appreciation is high as a result of forced memorizations, and we don't know that there is a great deal of value. Memorization is certainly inconsistent with modern education which emphasizes thought over rote.

However, children will inadvertently memorize poetry. Poems sung or spoken chorally become familiar. The responsive teacher will encourage his pupils to request favorite poems to be reread and reread. Thus, repetition in a meaningful, interesting way is likely to lead to a child's personal store of poetry. Poems in class booklets, poems posted around the room and the school may wind up in a child's memory. Memoriza-

---

[6]Association for Childhood Education. Literature Comm. *Sung Under the Silver Umbrella* (New York: Macmillan Co., 1939). Introduction, p. ix.

tion should be allowed to come naturally as a result of experience or personal choice, if it is to come at all.

Poetry Around and About

The visual availability of poetry further extends the poetry environment. One school has a bulletin board that always has a poem on it. There is nothing fancy about it; it is simply a poem lettered in large and readable script. The fact that it is there speaks for the commitment of staff and administration to poetry.

Within the classroom, such a simple idea could easily be implemented. An easel or wall space could be devoted to a poem, changed regularly. Attractive bulletin boards that vary in content should be planned. Some could have poems and illustrations, others could focus on a poet. Another approach would be to put up a bulletin board that stimulates the child to think about or to write poetry. Many ideas for encouraging creative writing could be presented visually and perhaps have greater impact by being available for a longer period of time.

Above all, there should be space for children who want to share with the rest of the class their own writing or poems they've discovered. A book of poems collected by the children, and constantly added to, is likely to be found in any situation where interest in poetry is sincere and deep.

The teacher might consider a poetry corner. Granted, a room can have just so many interest centers. But some kind of space will no doubt be found if a teacher considers the topic important enough! He can display books of poems including those locally published and produced; recordings of a wide range of poetry; pictures, objects, and questions that invite writers. Writing paper, pencils, erasers, and drawing materials should not be forgotten. For older children, the teacher might consider a bibliography of other poetry materials they might enjoy, and that are accessible but not kept in the classroom. (Children are particularly responsive to book covers.) It is a good idea to have available a set of stimulating questions for the child who is ready to be stimulated. The contents of this poetry corner should be in a constant state of flux, and the pupils should be involved in contributing to the corner.

Poetry and Visual Arts

Art and poetry belong together. Illustrators have proven this in many poetry books. Photography as an art is increasingly used to complement poetry. Richard Lewis and Harry Behn have called on photography for reproductions of original art in their collections of poetry of other cultures. Other books use photographs specifically chosen for that particular collection.

We can do a lot more to see and use relationships between art and poetry, as well as music and dance. For one thing, a discussion with children on these relationships should be very fruitful. All the arts should have rhythm, harmony, and unity. They represent the embodiment of an experience or of some part of an experience. A creator has made each from raw materials (scales, body movements, words, paper, paint, chalk, etc.), using his skill, imagination, and perception. All have the power to communicate to others. Their effects on those communicated with may be similar.

Combining the study of art, music, and poetry may be very appropriate at some time. Increasing emphasis is being placed on the humanities in education, and more effective approaches are needed. Perhaps the teacher can capitalize on these natural associations and work out new teaching strategies for the fine arts.

Art reproductions and originals not only have generalized relationships to poetry, but specific examples that fit together can be discovered. Fine paintings of horses lead naturally, not only into simple, descriptive poems about horses, but possibly into a poem such as "Reverie" (from de la Mare's *Songs of Childhood*), which captures the grace of riding. "Minnie Morse" (from Starbird's *Don't Ever Cross a Crocodile*) is in another vein entirely; Minnie is the horse fanatic many of us know. Patricia Hubbell personifies "October" as a horse in *The Apple Vendor's Fair*.

Daugherty's "Frontier Painters," (*West of Boston*), should be introduced in connection with the paintings of Bodmer, Catlin, or Remington, as should the art of the frontier in a study of the American West.

Poems and art may share a mood rather than a common subject. Poems may appeal to the same senses as art. The visual image most easily comes to mind. But certainly, texture, odor, sound, and taste may all be suggested by either medium.

The teacher may introduce a picture to children and ask them to be on the lookout for poems that seem to go well with it. This technique should not be limited to representational art, nor should the suggested assignment be required of everyone or be given a limited amount of time. If sufficient art reproductions are available, the teacher can turn this request around and ask for pictures (or three-dimensional art) that seem to fit a poem he has introduced.

This should not be done as a treasure hunt, but rather, as a means of encouraging children to think and feel more deeply about what the poet (artist) seems to be saying and doing. Increasing awareness and sensitivity might be outcomes of such an activity. Some children might be more challenged by this than by a general invitation to poetry.

Certainly, poetry should lead into children's own art. In too many classrooms, this never gets past illustrating what happens in a poem that the teacher has read or that the child has found. Perhaps it would be more useful to think in terms of what poetry suggests. How does this poem make you feel? might be better motivation than factual illustration. What experience in your life does this remind you of? What happens after the poem ends? How can you express visually the rhythm of this poem?

The child's effort need not be representational. An emotional response might be more concerned with color and form than with realism. Nor should there be limitation by media or dimension.

Some poems raise questions, and the responses might well be made through art. In *There Is No Rhyme for Silver,* Eve Merriam has included "A Dream." In the poem, she asks what you would do if you had a day all your own to do completely as you liked. The child might be asked to respond through art, or orally, or in writing, if he prefers.

"These Things I Love" (from Hubbell's *The Apple Vendor's Fair*) can lead, not only to the song "These Are a Few of My Favorite Things" (*Sound of Music*), but to the child's own sharing of his favorite things.

A wonderfully evocative selection from Rachel Field's *Poems* is "Almost" which suggests things going on that can almost—but not quite —be seen and heard. The mental images summoned could stimulate an art project.

There are many possibilities for murals. *A Book of Americans* (Benet) and *The Pheasant on Route Seven* both are concerned with people. Each child could contribute the figure of a person he particularly liked. Going beyond the poet, other people who could well appear in the book but who don't, could be added.

A story poem could be visually interpreted by a class. Many books with unifying aspects (e.g., *Hailstones and Halibut Bones,* which is all about colors) could become a starting point for a mural. A poet and his work is another possibility for a group art project.

Children and photography should not be overlooked. Increasing numbers of schools are providing facilities for pupils to become involved in both still and moving picture photography. The teacher might challenge camera buffs in his class to see poetry in the pictures they take.

A teacher could discuss with older children the desirability of illustrating books of poetry. Should the poet's words be pictured for us? If so, to what extent? All poetry books? If the reader were asked to illustrate a given title, what would be his response? What technique(s) would he use? How would he determine this?

Physical Interpretations

Bodily response to poetry is another way to involve children and to increase interest and appreciation. This may take the form of dramatization (probably pantomime while the poem is read); literal movement as described in the poem; or an interpretation in movement of the poem. (At least one poetry specialist considers this exhibitionism!)

Appropriate poems may not be found so easily. This approach, or any other, should not be attempted unless good poetry that will be enhanced by such treatment can be found.

The march rhythms of "They're Changing the Guard at Buckingham Palace," the circular motion which speeds up and then slows down in Dorothy Baruch's "Merry-Go-Round" (found in Arbuthnot's *Time for Poetry*) invite the listener to participate.

"The Rabbit Skip" (from Brown's *Nibble Nibble*) and "On Our Way" (from Merriam's *Catch a Little Rhyme*) both concern animal movement that could be imitated. (See also Marie Hall Ets' *Just Me*, a picture book in which a child eagerly moves like the animals on his farm.)

This essentially imitative response is for younger children. Perhaps the teacher will use such a poem (among other things) to give pupils the chance to stretch and move about during a literature session.

Increasingly personal interpretation is necesary for this to be a valid activity. "Fingers" (from Merriam's *There Is No Rhyme for Silver*) just begs one to explore what he can do with his own fingers.

Poems about fog, shadows, trees, the wind, and animals (particularly cats) can be found. These offer the child a chance to move in terms of what the poet says, but also to go beyond this.

On a higher level, a child may express in movement his feeling of the totality of the poem. Essentially, this would be dance, with or without verbal accompaniment. (Vachel Lindsay's poems have long been danced.)

It is a good idea to work with the physical education and creative dramatics consultants to explore these possibilities. Again, here is an opportunity to integrate activities and to see relationships rather than differences.

Children need to feel free to respond physically. It seems that such an open response is the essence of childhood, but we don't necessarily encourage it in schools. The older the child, the more likely he is to be inhibited about freely expressing himself in space, and also, the longer it probably has been since he had experience in doing so.

Therefore, the teacher will have to work from simple to increasingly complex and expressive responses. In a situation in which children feel free to try, knowing that the teacher will accept and that classmates won't laugh, older children may be willing to explore poetry with their bodies. However, if it is found that children are too self-conscious for this kind of activity, then forcing the issue would be unwise. (Perhaps the methods of the sensitivity trainers would be useful in drawing out physical responses, since they are getting fantastic responses from adults, a really repressed group).

Dramatization is less likely to be painful. The first time the writer saw this technique used, fifth graders took the title parts in "Mrs. Snipkin and Mrs. Wobblechin" (*Time for Poetry*). Most of the class members eagerly volunteered after having heard the poem. Two boys were chosen to take the parts.

Some dramatizations may involve the whole class, not merely character solos. "They're Changing the Guard at Buckingham Palace" can be more than a response in rhythm. How do these soldiers feel to be guards? How would you show it? Do the soldiers march in only one direction?

Poetry and Music

On occasion, one might combine poetry, music, and rhythmic movement. The open teacher working with responsive children will find successful combinations to which children will relate.

Poems set to music can be found, but it may be that the teacher or his pupils can compose appropriate melodies themselves. A good melody captures the spirit of the poem. How does this poem move? How does it make you feel? With what musical instrument(s) would it sound right? What kind(s) of voice(s) can you imagine singing it? Such questions may help children dig into a poem and more thoughtfully translate it into music.

It is suggested that the teacher seek out instrumental music that fits poems with which he enjoys working. Like art, the relationship could be that of mutual topic (the America of Copland and the America found in *West of Boston* or *A Book of Americans*). More so, the feelings engendered by a poem are similarly reflected in a musical composition. What poems remind the reader of Bach? Of jazz? The spareness of primitive poetry is reminiscent of plain songs. *Beyond the High Hills*, *Art of the Eskimo*, Eskimo music, and Eskimo folklore could be presented together in a moving way.

Working out musical accompaniments that seem to the child to fit a poem could be another way to integrate music, poetry, and meaning.

One group of college students used music in connection with *Hailstones and Halibut Bones*. They played selections from recordings and then asked the listeners what colors this music made them think of.

At this point, it might be well to repeat that poetry activities should serve to bring children and poetry together in such a way that children become increasingly interested in poetry and that they acquire ability to respond to it more and more fully. One can get so involved in clever ways to present poetry that he loses sight of his basic objectives. If such activities do the things we want to do with children, they are useful. When they are overused or forced, the purpose is defeated. We come back to the sensitive teacher who has good taste and judgment. The major presentation of poetry to children will be by oral reading, and the environment will provide materials, time, and climate for continuing enjoyment of poetry.

Learning about Poetry as a Literary Genre

Many of the activities and questions already mentioned suggest how one might "teach" poetry. Over-analysis of poems is, of course, to be avoided, as is the one-correct-interpretation theory. How can children be guided to a greater understanding of poetry as a genre and maintain their joy in poetry?

While watching basketball games during the period in which she had been writing this book, the author kept thinking of an analogy between poetry and basketball. She could follow the obvious actions in basketball, but everything else about the game was a blank. She could join in the cheering when a basket was made by her team; but often, she couldn't understand why the ball changed hands, or why the crowd was reacting as it was. If she had known more about the game, she would have understood more. She could then have interpreted nuances on the floor and in the bleachers, and she could have anticipated calls and moves. She could have discriminated between good playing and poor, and in all, basketball would have been more satisfying entertainment.

While poetry and basketball cannot be learned in the same way, it would seem that knowledge and experience are necessary to a true and full appreciation of each.

Little has been done to systematize the use and study of poetry in the elementary school. Huck and Kuhn's "A Taxonomy of Literary Understandings and Skills" (found in *Children's Literature in the Elementary School*) suggests an understanding of types of literature, components of poetry (meaning, imagery, diction, sound effects, forms), and the ability to evaluate literature.

A talk by Dr. Robert Carlsen is cited in *Elementary English*[7] in which he suggests five levels of appreciation of poetry. The first is the enjoyment of elements of sound and story; then recognition in poetry of

---

[7]Patricia Jean Cianciolo and Virginia M. Reid, "What Is Children's Literature? IV. Poetry for Today's Children," *Elementary English 41* (May 1964), 484-491. Also found in Virginia M. Reid, "Children's Literature—Old and New." (Champaign, Ill.: National Council of Teachers of English, 1964).

the child's own experiences; next, going beyond the world he lives in. Ability to understand symbolism and meanings below the surface, and an appreciation for patterns of writing and style complete the list.

The University of Nebraska has included a publication on poetry in its elementary language-literature-composition program. There is some information about poetry, and sample lesson plans are included, but primarily, it is an anthology of poems.[8]

The teacher should present lots of poetry to children before he starts worrying very much about poetry as literature. Certainly, the level of the children with whom he works will make a difference. There are questions that can be asked at any age to heighten children's understanding and enjoyment of poetry. Questions of this sort might be tried:

What is poetry?

Why do people write poetry?

Why do you think the author said this in a poem?

How does this poem make you feel?

Why do you think the poet used these words to describe the _____?

What words would you have used?

What senses does the author appeal to in this poem?

What do you notice about this poem?

Listen to the *sound* of the words as I read this poem. What do they make you think of? (Use to develop awareness of the suggestive sound of language.)

Here is a poem about a person. Does he seem real to you? Why?

What picture does this poem bring to your mind? sounds? smells? etc.

What does the poet say that stimulates this picture? sound? smell?

What do *you* think the poet is saying? (The reason for such a question is to encourage children to interpret for themselves and let the poem speak to them. *It Doesn't Always Have to Rhyme* [Merriam] has several poems that relate to the fact that the interpretation of a poem is very personal. "What Did You Say?" says that a poem is for *you*. "Mona Lisa" says that it is you who determines the meaning.)

Compare these poems, both about the same thing, for example, Aiken's "The Grasshopper" in *Cats and Bats and Things with Wings* and McCord's "The Grasshopper" in *Far and Few*.

What do you notice about limericks (haiku, etc.)? Keep your eyes open to see if you are right.

Now that we've read quite a few of his poems, what kind of person do you think this poet may be?

---

[8] *A Curriculum for English: Poetry for the Elementary Grades.* (Lincoln, Neb.: University of Nebraska Press, 1966).

Why do many poets use rhyme? What is good about using it? What is bad about using rhyme?[9]

What do you notice about the way in which rhyme is used in this poem? (Perhaps the teacher will present several poems at a time with different rhyme schemes and introduce a variety over a period of time. This is not an exercise in matching words but an indication that rhyme can be used in many ways for many purposes and that poets are experimenting with new ways. A good poet uses more than one rhyme scheme.)

Here is a word that the dictionary says means _____. This is the *denotative* meaning. In poetry, words are often chosen because of their *connotative* meaning. What does the word _____ make you think of? (The teacher might use words like family, tree, warm, sad, blue, telephone, sleep. For younger children, he can begin to develop the concept without actually using the words *denotative* and *connotative*. He might try "Mean Song" from Merriam's *There Is No Rhyme for Silver,* and Lewis Carroll's "Jabberwocky." These abound with nonsense words that have only connotative meanings.)

Why is it that we can sing this poem?

Is this a poem? Why, or why not?

Many teachers use parodies or poor examples to help children discover what skill the good poet employs. How could this poem be improved? Compare a purposely poor parody with its original.

Some teachers have had their pupils "translate" a poem into prose, and then compare the two versions; or read a factual statement about something, then a poem on the same subject, and compare the two.

Such questioning, used sparingly and pertinently, can go far beyond mere presentation in developing awareness and appreciation of poetics. This need not be a step-by-step procedure; practically all the suggested questions could be asked in some form at any age level. It is advisable to use questions and activities as they seem to have timeliness and validity in order to stimulate children to go beyond the surface of a poem. It is best not to ask very many questions at a time.

Children will think about and discuss poems when we give them a chance to do so. An atmosphere that is open to reaction and comment may produce more than the best worded of questions. When the children spark the talking, our questioning may be limited toward turning their thoughts in directions they had not discovered themselves.

Teachers would do well to utilize the work of educators who are involved with creative thinking and questioning technique. They have

---

[9]With older children, the teacher might want to share suitable professional readings. Children might better be able to discuss rhyme after exposure to an article such as: Patrick Groff, "Take Time For Rhyme," *Elementary English* 40 (November 1963), 762-764.

much to say philosophically and practically about working with children to provide much more creative, thought-provoking activities in the classroom.

Writing Poetry

The writing of poetry is an integral part of the poetry program. Certainly, children learn much about the art of poetry through their own efforts to write. More important than all the approaches used is the environment which not only encourages, but invites children to write poetry. A room where children are exposed to rich experiences (not only in language), where openness is encouraged and honesty sought, where time and materials are made available for writing, where children know that their writing will be accepted, is one in which all children are likely to try their hand at writing.

The perceptive, emotional aspects of what a child writes are more important than structure. And yet he must ultimately work within structure if he is to write poetry. Thus writing and understanding poetry are intertwined.

Children should see themselves not as imitators of those who write poetry, but as poets themselves. There are too many examples of dah-de-dah verse, where the concept of poetry seems to be limited to strict rhythm and rhyme. This is why, if a choice must be made, a child's honest expression is preferred to structure.

Since poetry is built on words, activities that call attention to words should be helpful. An excellent source for ideas is Alastair Reid's *Ounce Dice Trice*.[10] This is a collection of words, practically any page of which could be used as a starting point for lively sharing of vocabulary. There are heavy words, light words, names for whales, homemade onomatopoeia (scissors on paper: "tris-tras"), a new counting system, words strung in garlands (tingle-airey to piddocks to breastsummer . . .). It's a marvelous vehicle for having fun with words and for developing awareness of words as meaning, sounds, connotations.

A small picture book entitled *A Hole Is to Dig*[11] can lead from single words to phrases. The teacher can read enough of the "definitions" for children to get the feel of the book. Then he should stop short and let them complete the definitions in their own way, for example, "A cat is to . . ." This gives opportunity for expression of thoughts and feelings.

---

[10]Alastair Reid, *Ounce Dice Trice*. Drawings by Ben Shahn. (Boston: Little, Brown & Co., 1958).

[11]Ruth Krauss, *A Hole Is to Dig*. Illustrated by Maurice Sendak. (New York: Harper & Row, 1952).

Some teachers list all the ideas children suggest in response to a topic. Then the children mold these ideas into a poem by rearranging the order of words and phrases, changing words, adding, taking away, so that the poem not only says what they feel, but sounds pleasing and poetic.

Imagery in poetry can be introduced by asking children to finish old sayings in new ways. At least for older children, "A Cliché" (from Merriam's *It Doesn't Always Have to Rhyme*) is a fine introduction. What are fresher ways to say "as quiet as a mouse"?

Nancy Larrick also suggests the unfinished sentence. Children can be asked to complete sentences like "The howling wind. . . ," "The bright sunlight. . . ," "The spicy stew. . . ," "The mysterious chest. . . ," all of which begin to suggest a sensory image.

The teacher and children might talk about words and their shades of meaning. What can you use for the word *walk* (used as a verb)? Which would be best in a given situation? a given sentence?

What words could you use to describe a tree? that tree in autumn? in winter? The teacher can bring in things which he asks children to describe, for example, fabrics, sound effects, art objects, living things, incense. He can give them things to taste or feel and ask for their reactions. He might try art-op and pop, psychedelic lighting, Indian music. Children should be turned on to feelings and words.

All of these techniques have two overwhelming advantages: they avoid trapping children in the overemphasis on rhyme, and they ease children into writing poetry. The child who scoffs at or fears writing poetry is very likely to participate in such open-ended talk.

Simply allowing time after a poetry reading session to let children try their hand at writing will produce poetry. Poetry on demand is something else. A child will write when he is ready, and not simply because we are ready for him to do so. Poems are not an assignment to be handed in after twenty minutes.

A student teacher recently submitted her experience with poetry writing and some of the results. Much of it is derivative, but all the poems show some spark of originality and understanding of poetry.

"During the spring semester of 1969, I was assigned to do my student teaching experience in the fifth grade at Riverview School in Elkhart, Indiana. My cooperating teacher was Eugene Thomas; the principal was Andre Cummins. The classroom was organized into learning centers. My fifth graders proved not only to be highly responsible and independent workers, but also very creative. There was quite a spontaneous and free-flowing atmosphere throughout the class of twenty-four pupils. In a combination literature-creative writing lesson, I introduced some of Carl Sandburg's works, then encouraged the children to

write their own poetry, stressing to them that the lines did not have
to rhyme. A list of five topics was suggested, but they were free to write
on any subject. Some children wrote more than one poem, others illustrated their poems, while others felt lucky just to get their poems
written."[12]

OUTSIDE

Apples are red like roses,
Tulips are blue like love,
They are all around me.

Julie App

PEPPER

Pepper, pepper
Makes you sneeze.
Ice cream, ice cream,
Chills your teeth!

Annette Warren

BABY

Slippery,
  gushy,
    wet, oh wet.
Oh, baby, quit that splashing.
But baby didn't stop.
Splash
  slap
    crack.
  Baby hit me.
I swallowed the bar of soap and
  all I hear is
    goo goo gah gah!
Is that any way
  for a college
    kid to act.

Michael Fahlbeck

THE SEA

The sea is very calm,
And the sea is also big,
The sea can also be very small,
But nobody
  Can change the sea
    But God.

Cristina Truex

---

[12]Frances M. Bussard, Elkhart, Indiana. Purdue undergraduate in elementary
education.

SUMMER

Summer is sometimes warm,
Summer is sometimes cool,
Summer is here and
My brother is a year old.

Sherri Mahan

SUNSET

In the evening the sun is set high,
And I watch it go down behind a hill
The hill is very tall and the sun goes
Down fast as I watch it go
Down behind the tall hill.

Shirley Chapman

SUN

Sun is fun,
Fun is joy,
Joy is Happiness,
Happiness is sun.

Mark Scher

BLOCK BUSTERS

The men in Vietnam
All fight for us,
They help our country
In war to defend the
Nation's capital.

Bill Bohinc

ABOUT SCHOOL

Roses are red
Violets are blue
Down with teacher
And down with School.

Duane Krauter

It is a good idea to have a poetry box or folder where children can put their poetry when they are ready to share it, and for the teacher to be available to the child who asks him to read his poetry.

The use of pictures to motivate writing is widespread. *Stop, Look and Write!*[13] gives some very specific ideas for using photographs to develop powers of observation and to communicate through words what has been seen. Each of twenty sections highlights a topic, providing

---

[13]Hart Day Leavitt and David A. Sohn, *Stop, Look and Write!* (New York: Bantam Pathfinder Editions, 1964). Also of interest is Leavitt's *The Writer's Eye* (New York: Bantam Pathfinder Editions, 1968).

appropriate photographs, questions, and activities. Although aimed at creative writing in general, the emphasis on awareness and exciting use of words make this a most useful book.

Art reproductions, slides, pictures from magazines all may be used to stimulate writing. The pictures in *Stop, Look and Write* are the result of just such a personal collection. Pictures may also be used for oral reactions.

Can young children write poetry? Of course they can *make* poetry, but *we* may have to do the actual writing. A simply operated tape recorder that is always available may invite children to record their poems and ideas on the instant. Problems with writing or with losing spontaneity may be overcome by having handy and immediate outlets like this. One might consider the use of the recorder for taping class sessions when children talk about and try out poetry.

The teacher may move from talk to simple written descriptions of objects, thoughts, or experiences.

Children would probably enjoy experimenting with various forms of poetry. Haiku and cinquain are particularly popular. An excellent guide to the former is Harold Henderson's *Haiku in English* which gives a rich background for the appreciation and writing of haiku.

Sometimes one particular book of poems may appeal to a class. The children may be sufficiently interested to try writing poems that could be included in such a book. *A Book of Americans* has been known to motivate children to write more poems about our country and its people. Illustrated animal poems (not always with the author and the artist the same person) followed one class's enjoyment of *Cats and Bats and Things with Wings*.

A poem may suggest to the child something he'd like to write. In *A Book of Americans*, Nancy Hanks questions any listener about her son whose later life she doesn't foresee. Few could fail to respond in some fashion.

Creative writing certainly shouldn't be limited to poetry. Periods in which children are set loose to create — sculpture, illustration, prose, poetry, conversation, dramatization — should be regularly available. Children should be given time to share what they do with each other if they wish.

Our aim is to give children the chance and the motivation to write. We hope that they will and that the experience is satisfying enough that they will continue to write for the rest of their lives, whether often or only occasionally.

A collection of individual and classroom anthologies gives children the opportunity to share their own poems and those of published poets whose work is enjoyed. If such a collection becomes a routine instead of a joy, it ought to be discontinued.

Flora Arnstein, Hughes Mearns, and Natalie Cole all have written about the creative situation, where children think, speak, write, and act freely. These authors' works are readable and inspiring, and are highly recommended. More recently, Richard Lewis is emerging as a leader in the area of children's writing. His articles and collections should be sought out and prized.

Poetry is many things to many people. For children, it may be particularly rich and rewarding and have meaning for them that goes far beyond the pleasurable moment spent reading a poem. If we truly believe in humanity, in openness, in joy, in creativity, in giving children something to carry through life, we can do no less than to provide children constantly with meaningful poems and experiences with poetry, enriched by our love and enthusiasm for children and poetry.

Piping down the valleys wild,
    Piping songs of pleasant glee,
On a cloud I saw a child,
    And he laughing said to me:

"Pipe a song about a Lamb!"
    So I piped with merry chear,
"Piper, pipe that song again";
    So I piped: he wept to hear.

"Drop thy pipe, thy happy pipe;
    "Sing thy songs of happy chear:"
So I sung the same again,
    While he wept with joy to hear.

"Piper, sit thee down and write
    "In a book that all may read."
So he vanish'd from my sight,
    And I pluck'd a hollow reed,

And I made a rural pen,
    And I stain'd the water clear,
And I wrote my happy songs
    Every child may joy to hear.

William Blake

SELECTED REFERENCES

1. General Introductions to Children's Literature and Language Arts

ARBUTHNOT, MAY HILL. *Children and Books*. Chicago: Scott, Foresman & Co., 1964.

ARBUTHNOT, MAY HILL; CLARK, MARGARET MARY; and LONG, HAR-
RIET GENEVA. *Children's Books Too Good to Miss.* Cleveland:
Western Reserve University, 1966.

GEORGIOU, CONSTANTINE. *Children and Their Literature.* Englewood
Cliffs, N.J.: Prentice-Hall, 1969.

HOPKINS, LEE BENNETT. *Let Them Be Themselves.* New York: Cita-
tion Press, 1969.

HUCK, CHARLOTTE S., and KUHN, DORIS YOUNG. *Children's Literature in the Elementary School.* 2d ed. New York: Holt, Rinehart
& Winston, 1968.

JACOBS, LELAND B. *Using Literature with Young Children.* New York:
Teachers College Press, Teachers College, Columbia University,
1965.

LARRICK, NANCY. *A Parent's Guide to Children's Reading.* Garden
City, N.Y.: Doubleday & Co., 1969.

———. *A Teacher's Guide to Children's Books.* Columbus, Ohio:
Charles E. Merrill Books, 1960.

SMITH, LILLIAN H. *The Unreluctant Years.* Chicago: American Library
Association, 1953.

TIEDT, IRIS M. and SIDNEY W. *Contemporary English in the Elementary School.* Englewood Cliffs, N. J.: Prentice-Hall, 1967.

2. Books about Poetry and Creativity. (Examples of Children's Writings)

APPLEGATE, MAUREE. *Easy in English,* An Imaginative Approach to
the Teaching of Language Arts. New York: Harper & Row, 1960.

ARNSTEIN, FLORA J. *Children Write Poetry,* A Creative Approach.
New York: Dover Publications, n.d.

Most useful for the examples of poems written by children.
Arnstein's evolving philosophy, the techniques she uses to stimulate children, her evaluation of poetry, discussion of barriers of
freedom.

———. *Poetry in the Elementary Classroom,* A Publication of The
National Council of Teachers of English. New York: Appleton-
Century-Crofts, 1962.

How the author uses poetry. Less on writing, more on presentation. Many children's poems. Discussion of characteristics of
children's writing.

BEHN, HARRY. *Chrysalis,* Concerning Children and Poetry. New York:
Harcourt, Brace & World, 1968.

BURROWS, ALVINA TREUT; JACKSON, DORIS C.; and SAUNDERS, DOR-
OTHY O. *They All Want to Write,* Written English in the Elementary School. 3d ed. New York: Holt, Rinehart & Winston,
1964.

CHUKOVSKY, KORNEI. *From Two to Five.* MIRIAM MORTON, trans.
and ed. Foreword by FRANCES CLARKE SAYERS. Berkeley, Calif.:
University of California Press, 1968.

A discussion, with humorous examples, of the unfettered language
of young children. Several chapters are directly concerned with
poetry.

COLE, NATALIE ROBINSON. *The Arts in the Classroom.* Photographs by C. K. EATON. New York: John Day Co., 1940.

A classic work in the literature of the creativists. Author's experiences with painting, claywork, print-making, free rhythmic dancing, and creative writing (prose) are described. Its value is that it adds to a philosophy of creativity.

DANBY, JOHN T. *Approach to Poetry.* New York: James H. Heinemann, 1940.

Ideas for "teaching" poetry, many of which are sound.

FORD, BORIS, ed. *Young Writers, Young Readers,* An Anthology of Children's Reading and Writing. London: Hutchinson of London, 1960, 1963.

HENDERSON, HAROLD. *Haiku in English.* Rutland, Vt.: Charles E. Tuttle Co., 1967.

JOSEPH, STEPHEN M., ed. *The Me Nobody Knows,* Children's Voices from the Ghetto. New York: Avon Books, 1969.

Life Through Young Eyes, A Collection of Children's Art, Poetry and Prose. Aylesbury, England: Dolphin Publishing Co., 1960.

LOWENFELD, VIKTOR. *Creative and Mental Growth.* 4th ed. New York: Macmillan Co., 1964.

MCCASLIN, NELLIE. *Creative Dramatics in the Classroom.* New York: David McKay Co., 1968.

Development of a creative dramatics program, with one chapter on poetry.

MEARNS, HUGHES. *Creative Power.* The Education of Youth in the Creative Arts. Introduction by WINIFRED WARD. 2d rev. ed. New York: Dover Publications, 1958.

Mearns has been in the forefront of the creative movement. In a very readable way, he tells of his experiences with children and young people in helping them develop as creative people.

———. *Creative Youth.* Garden City, N.Y.: Doubleday & Co., 1929.

SIKS, GERALDINE BRAIN. *Children's Literature for Dramatization,* An Anthology. New York: Harper & Row, 1964.

Offers casual suggestions for use, but one must go elsewhere for technique. First three chapters: Poetry Inviting Action, Poetry Inviting Characterization, Poetry Motivating Conflict. Each poem has a brief introduction giving background, suggesting possible approaches which are, most often, questions and related music.

WALTERS, NINA. *Let Them Write Poetry.* New York: Holt, Rinehart & Winston, 1962.

WARD, WINIFRED. *Playmaking with Children,* From Kindergarten through Junior High School. 2d ed. New York: Appleton-Century-Crofts, 1957.

The philosophy of creativity, the interrelationships of arts.

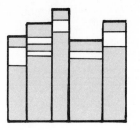

index